BEL
BA

CW01646161

Christian Baptism — its theology and practice

Gordon W. Kuhrt

MOWBRAY
LONDON & OXFORD

Copyright © Gordon W. Kuhrt 1987

First published 1987
by A. R. Mowbray & Co. Ltd,
Saint Thomas House, Becket Street,
Oxford, OX1 1SJ

All rights reserved. No part of this publication may be reproduced, stored in a retrieval system, or transmitted in any form or by any means, electronic, mechanical, photocopying, recording, or otherwise, without the prior permission in writing from the publisher, A. R. Mowbray & Co. Ltd.

Typeset by Spire Print Services Ltd., Salisbury
Printed in Great Britain by Biddles Ltd., Guildford

British Library Cataloguing in Publication Data

Kuhrt, Gordon W.
Believing in baptism : Christian baptism — its theology and practice.
1. Baptism
I. Title
265′.1 BV811.2

ISBN 0-264-67088-4

Contents

Preface

Confusion about baptism is obvious and widespread. This book is the result of pleas by clergy and ordinands for a single volume that treats coherently the major issues. I am grateful for encouraging response to lectures and seminars throughout England, and in January 1987 in Pakistan and South India.

The numerous booklets by Bishop Colin Buchanan have exercised a great influence, and I gladly acknowledge my indebtedness. He and other friends have read parts of the manuscript and made valuable criticisms Roger Beckwith, Leslie Houlden, John Balchin, Wilfred Kuhrt. My colleague David Richardson contributed both encouragement and many helpful suggestions. My secretary Valerie Gower typed with great accuracy. I am deeply grateful to each of them.

Baptism is a precious gift of God, in the name of Jesus, and in the Spirit. I pray this book will bring glory to the triune God, and assist in making disciples, baptising and teaching them (Matthew 28.19–20).

G. W. K.

Acknowledgements

1. Bible quotations are from the New International Version © 1978 by the New York International Bible Society published in the UK by Hodder & Stoughton Ltd. and are used by permission
2. Extracts from the Book of Common Prayer of 1662 which is Crown Copyright in the United Kingdom, are reproduced by permission of Eyre and Spottiswood (Publishers) Ltd., Her Majesty's Printers, London.
3. Extracts from the Alternative Service Book 1980 are reproduced by permission of the Central Board of Finance of the Church of England.
4. The Canons of the Church of England are published by the Church Information Office and extracts are reproduced by permission of the Central Board of Finance of the Church of England.

1
Who believes in baptism?

'Believing in baptism' can be taken in two ways. Firstly, it may refer to the element of faith when a person is baptized. Who has to have faith, what kind of faith, and when must they hold it? Secondly, it may refer to the importance of baptism for the Christian Church as a whole. Do we think baptism is important? Why do we practise it, and who is it for? In both these senses believing in baptism raises important and perplexing issues for the Church today.

Believing?

The major issue in the theology of baptism today is the necessity and nature of '*believing* faith'. At what point should there be 'believing' with respect to baptism, and how should it be demonstrated? 'The necessity of faith for the reception of the salvation embodied and set forth in baptism is acknowledged by all the churches' says the influential World Council of Churches report *Baptism, Eucharist and Ministry* (cited in future as *BEM*)[1] But with regard to how baptism, faith and salvation are related to each other, the churches are deeply divided not only between each other but also internally.

All Christian churches who practise baptism at all will baptize a 'believer' who comes from another religion or from unbelief. This will take place following a personal confession of faith, but how is this 'believing' to be judged? At what age is a child able to make a (credible, personal, responsible) profession? Should the baptism even of an adult be immediate as seems to have been the case usually in the Acts of the Apostles, or should there be careful preparation over weeks or even months?

The Church of England Alternative Service Book requires an explicit three-fold affirmation of faith from those to be baptized who are old enough to answer for themselves, and also from the parents and sponsors (godparents) of those not old enough. The statements of the liturgy may well be impeccable:

Do you believe and trust in God the Father who made the world?
Answer: I believe and trust in him.
Do you believe and trust in his Son Jesus Christ, who redeemed mankind?
Answer: I believe and trust in him.
Do you believe and trust in his Holy Spirit, who gives life to the people of God?
Answer: I believe and trust in him.[2]

but *BEM* still found it necessary to say that those who practise infant baptism 'must guard themselves against the practice of apparently indiscriminate baptism and take more seriously their responsibility for the nurture of baptized children to mature commitment to Christ'.[3]

For all Christians then who practise baptism there are today issues concerning 'believing' in baptism with respect to its timing, its reality, its maturity and its credibility.

Baptism?

However, (and this is the *second* meaning of the title) there are Christians today for whom believing in *baptism* itself is (or at least seems to be) of very little importance at all. The Society of Friends (known as Quakers) do not practise baptism with water or holy communion with bread and wine as rites of material signs, but seek to practise 'a sacramental life through the living presence of Christ'.[4] Similarly the Salvation Army accept as church members 'all those who are in Christ Jesus'[5] without any rite of initiation by water-baptism.

Surprisingly, moreover, many Baptist Churches too make baptism an entirely voluntary and personal matter and accept people into membership and to Holy Communion who are unbaptized. Other Christians will be found worshipping in various congregations and having a living faith in God but who cannot see the point of the sign of water-baptism when they have experienced the reality of spiritual baptism. This attitude is often associated with an individualistic and pietistic form of Christianity. There are African Churches which practise baptism of the Holy Spirit without water, through the laying on of hands. But there are also many other Christians who do believe and practise water-baptism but see it as much less significant than 'conversion' or 'baptism with the Spirit'. The one is a *sign* (whether it seems to come before or after what it signifies) while the other is the *reality*! Often the sign and the reality are separated by weeks, months or many years, and it is the reality (quite understandably) that is prayed and worked for and rejoiced over in the church, while the sign is but a shadow in comparison.

Then there are many churches where baptism is apparently regarded in theological terms as highly significant in relation to the gospel and the church of Jesus Christ, and yet most baptisms take place at semi-private services when few (if any) of the church members are present. Or again, parents and sponsors make professions of faith but are never seen in the congregation again (until another baptism — or perhaps wedding or funeral) and appear to have little intention of truly bringing the children up 'as Christians within the family of the Church'. Is this believing in baptism?

A biblical theology

The purpose of this book is to enquire carefully into the biblical theology of baptism. This will involve an understanding of the nature of conversion, repentance and faith. There can be only 'one baptism' — as there is 'one body and one Spirit, one hope, one Lord, one faith, one God and Father of all' (Ephesians 4.4–6). So there is one theology of Christian baptism which we must endeavour to clarify from the Scriptures. Having done that (and only then) we shall turn to the thorny issue of Christian family baptism (or paedo-baptism) — the view that it is right to baptize the infants of Christian parents, and to the 'baptist' view that any infant baptism is misguided.

It would be a theological nonsense for readers to jump to chapters 7 and 8 without working through the earlier chapters — however, when that point is reached, the author believes the biblical theology points quite clearly to a particular conclusion. He is concerned though to be 'eirenical' to those who interpret the evidence differently, and to face the pastoral questions of discipline and 're-baptism' in a scrupulous and serious manner.

The book is not intended to be a piece of academic research and so notes and references will be kept to a minimum. It is intended to be a careful and clear enquiry which produces a coherent account, biblically reasoned and pastorally applicable. This point is emphasized because so much of the literature on this subject is on the one hand densely academic, technical and detailed, or on the other hand either very superficial or bitterly polemical and partisan. It is written not for the professional scholar but for clergy, ministers, ordinands and that growing band of lay people who gladly help with baptism preparation, administration and subsequent nurture but are perplexed as to the real meaning and importance of the whole enterprise.

A changing scene

Changing contexts have a marked effect on the priorities and practice of theological reflection — whether we are always conscious of it or not. It is helpful to note certain developments during the past generation or so which have particular significance for the discussion and practice of Christian initiation —

1. The western world is increasingly seen to be a *secularized mission-field* rather than part of Christendom. In 1981 the number of Christians in third-world countries surpassed that of the western world[6] and the trends of growth and decline respectively continue. There is consequently a move among perceptive church leadership from the pastoral to the evangelistic. This is more talked-about than acted-upon but it is a real part of the agenda in an increasingly demanding way. The decline in church membership must either lead to massive retrenchment or to major re-tooling for mission.

Bishops, clergy and lay leaders are still primarily trained for and confident in pastoral care rather than evangelism. But the change is coming! A feature which is delaying the change in some circles is anxiety about the propriety of Christian evangelism at all especially in a multi-faith society. Much more work is needed on the biblical theology of evangelism, conversion and salvation. This is not the place — except to urge a new confidence in the Great Commission from the risen Lord Jesus who placed baptism firmly in the context of mission to all nations, the proclamation of good news, making disciples and teaching the Faith (Matthew 28.19–20).[7]

A healthy church will hold together its pastoral, social and teaching ministry with its evangelistic mission. Churches in the third world increasingly show the way. Adult baptisms are becoming a very significant feature in the life of the Church of England. It seems very probable that far more adults (i.e. those over 18) are being baptized each year in the Church of England than in the Baptist Union Churches.[8]

2. *Biblical theology* is more influential in theological discussion and in church life than for several generations past. This is because of the inadequacies of theological liberalism, the contributions of the 'biblical theology' movement, the rise in numbers, confidence and theological integrity of evangelicals, the pervasive spirituality of the Charismatic movement and the unlocking of doors by the Second Vatican Council. The World Council of Churches is 'a fellowship of churches which confess the Lord Jesus Christ as God and Saviour *according to the scriptures* and therefore seek to fulfil together their common calling to the glory of the one God, Father, Son and Holy Spirit'. *The Anglican-Roman Catholic International Commission Final Report* says, 'Since the Scriptures are the uniquely inspired witness to divine revelation, the Church's expression of that revelation must be tested by its consonance with Scripture'.[9]

When this criterion is applied to baptism, there is a decisive shift from a pragmatic to a principled approach.

3. There is increasing *pressure for agreed policies of discipline* and discrimination. The involvement of lay people in evangelism and in baptism preparation means that many church councils are discussing baptism policy. Co-operative ministries between churches

of the same or different denominations require agreement about procedures, and every few years there are attempts in various dioceses and in General Synod to clarify Church of England policy. No longer is it a private matter for the clergy or a private matter for a local church — it is a *Church* issue, which means laity and other churches cannot be ignored. The ecumenical movement, and especially the publication of the study paper 'Baptism, Eucharist and Ministry', has enabled many Christians to study the issues and hear about other approaches in a dramatically new way.

4. The teaching and experience of *baptism in the Spirit* has become commonplace in the wake of Pentecostalism and the Charismatic movement. Even where this is not seen as an essentially second or further experience subsequent to water-baptism and/or conversion, it has resulted in a raising of spiritual consciousness. There is a more vivid awareness that the Christ (the Anointed with the Spirit One) comes to 'baptize with the Holy Spirit'. This has a great significance for thinking about baptism generally.

5. The expectation of *a 're-baptism'* in some of the Restorationist 'House-churches', and the request for a baptism-by-immersion by some (especially young people) who have been baptized as babies is a major theological/pastoral issue in many areas. Although the issue has always been around, it is sharper now than ever before, and is another significant context for our theological enquiry.

Where shall we start

We all approach this issue with a particular personal history which does or does not include experience of particular teaching and practices of baptism. Furthermore such teaching and experience might have been found personally helpful or unhelpful. It might have been in the context of a welcoming Christian community or an apparently harsh and unloving one. It might have been presented by an approachable, kindly clergyman or an apparently too-busy, uncaring one. It might have been in the context of thoughtful biblical teaching or an apparent appeal to tradition, church rules and Canon Law. Finally, it might have been considered in a careful, leisured, rational way through sermon, preparation class, lecture or book, or in the highly emotional contexts of either adult or peer pressure in adolescence or immediately following the birth of a baby and 'wanting it done' or being under pressure by grand-parents to 'have it christened and named proper'. The controversies over infant baptism — whether it is ever right or not, and whether it should be administered with careful discrimination or not — cast their shadows over any study of baptism.

So every reader will be coming with a different experience and a different agenda of questions, problems and expectations. It is often asserted that 'we must start where people are' — and that is usually important in personal conversation and counselling. When preaching to or teaching a group, however, the audience may consist of people who are at many different places in their thinking and experience — so too with a book. For this reason we shall not start with considerations of *psychology* or *sociology.* These issues will play some part later on — the psychology of the child and the teenager is significant in pastoral issues of initiation and nurture, and the sociology of peer pressure on the adolescent and on new parents is very relevant too.

Neither shall we start with *church law* or the situation of church policy and practice now. Churches differ widely on these matters, and even within the same denomination there are widely divergent interpretations and practice, It is not an issue that divides neatly along other theological or ecclesiastical lines — for instance it cuts right across the liberal/evangelical, the catholic/protestant, the established/free-church and the 'charismatic-issue' divisions.

Nor shall we start with a consideration of baptism in *church history*. It is an immensely complex and tangled story and the interpretation of initiation in the second century and following periods of the early church is a matter of considerable controversy. The debates have usually generated more heat than light.

Neither shall we start with a consideration of *sacramental theology* — the relation between a 'sign' and the 'thing signified' and issues of validity (is it real?) and of efficacy (is it effective?). These have been matters of major controversy with respect to both baptism and holy communion. Also controversial is the extent to which other rites or ceremonies (such as confirmation, marriage, ordination, confession and unction) are sacraments. We shall later consider the value and significance of the term 'sacrament', but it is not a biblical term, and is loaded with overtones of centuries of controversy — not a good place to start!

This enquiry will begin unambiguously with the biblical evidence — while recognizing that quite inevitably we shall all look at that evidence through 'spectacles' misted (more or less) by our own personal experience. God the Father, his Son Jesus Christ and the Holy Spirit are made known in a uniquely clear way in the Christian Scriptures. They enable people to understand 'salvation through faith in Christ Jesus'. They are 'God-breathed' and 'useful for teaching, rebuking, correcting and training in righteousness, so that the man of God may be thoroughly equipped for every good work' (2 Timothy 3.15–16). 'Prophecy never had its origin in the will of man, but men spoke from God as they were carried along by the Holy Spirit' (2 Peter 1.21).

Different churches have interpreted Scripture differently, and various theological systems have given varying emphasis to the place of tradition, church authority, human reason or conscience and the experienced guidance of the Holy Spirit in a particular situation. However, the overwhelming majority of Christians throughout history, and all major Confessions of Faith, acknowledge unambiguously the unique and normative authority of Scripture for Christian faith. Article VI of the Church of England says 'Holy Scripture contains all things necessary to salvation: so that whatever is not read therein, nor may be proved thereby, is not to be required of any man, that it should be believed as an Article of the Faith, or be requisite or necessary to salvation'.

True Christian unity will only be developed with integrity on the basis of going back to the biblical roots and foundation, and sharing in honest and painstaking enquiry about what God said by his prophets and apostles through his Spirit then, and what he is saying through the Scripture and the Spirit now. The two horizons of 'then' and 'now' must be brought together. God's word is to be a lamp to our feet, and a light for our path (Psalm 119.105).

2

The Bible and baptism

The problem of where to start is only partially dealt with by turning first to the Bible. The controversy over the legitimacy of infant baptism has polarized those who begin in the Old Testament (because the Bible starts there, and the whole Bible, not just the second part, is Christian Scripture) and those who turn straight to the New Testament (because there Jesus commanded baptism, and there the apostles explained it as union with Christ in his death and resurrection).

Later in this chapter a way through this procedural dilemma will become clearer. It will be seen that the apostles in their Epistles understand baptism in the light of the Old Testament revelation of God's covenant.

First though we note the remarkable number of approaches by different scholars.

Varieties of approach

1. Some begin with alleged *antecedents of Christian baptism*. These may be *Jewish circumcision* — but often the question is begged about how and why circumcision and baptism relate, the relationship of Old and New Testament to each other generally, and the nature of the 'new covenant'; the use of water in religious ceremonies generally, and particularly in *Jewish rituals of purification* — but there is no unequivocally direct line between these and Christian baptism; *Jewish proselyte baptism* whereby non-Jews, male and female, underwent a water-ceremony to make them 'children of the covenant' — but there is

still controversy over the date of its development, and no clear reference to it in the New Testament. These are all significant issues, and the first two antecedents are clearly biblical. However, starting the enquiry with circumcision is often seen as trying to answer the question about infant baptism before the nature of Christian baptism has been examined properly at all. It is methodologically debatable, and ecumenically divisive.

2. Other scholars begin where the New Testament begins, with the very obvious antecedent of Christian baptism in the *baptism of John*, the forerunner of the Messiah. This is of great importance to the apostles who make frequent references to it, but it is quite clearly pre-Christian. It does not incorporate two of the distinctive features of Christian baptism, which is 'into Christ' and associated with 'baptism of the Holy Spirit'. John himself contrasted sharply his own baptism with *water*, and the subsequent Messianic baptism with *Spirit*. John's ministry of baptism is highly significant but is not the key to understanding the meaning of Christian baptism.

3. It seems much more promising to begin at *the baptism of Jesus* himself. Although this baptism is by John and part of his general programme of baptizing, it has dramatically new features. Jesus (owned as God's Son by the voice from heaven) is at the centre of the episode, and the Holy Spirit descends on him in a clear and dramatic manner. Surely the example of Jesus at the outset of his public ministry is the pattern for a believer at the outset of his or her Christian life and ministry. Attractive and suggestive though this is (and it will be expounded in chapters 5 and 11) it must be also noted that distinctive features of Christian baptism are not obviously present. Christian baptism is 'into Christ', involves assurance of forgiveness and marks incorporation into God's

people. These features are not in the baptism of Jesus, and indicate that this is a unique event which bridges between the baptism of John and the ministry of Jesus which will culminate in Christian baptism. It is only after the death and resurrection of the Messiah and the Pentecostal outpouring of the Spirit that Christian baptism in its fullness can be known. There are brief references to Jesus and his disciples exercising a ministry of baptism themselves (John 3.22, 26; 4.1–2) but no details are given, and no particular teaching or significance is attached to it. It is probably best seen as an extension and affirmation of John's ministry of proclaiming the need of spiritual reality and decisive action in the light of God's kingdom-reign.

4. Others assert that the very foundation of Christian baptism is to be found only in the *death and resurrection of Jesus Christ.*[1] One must be born of 'water and Spirit' (John 3.5), and the decisive link between the water (of John's baptism) and the Spirit (of Christian baptism) is to be found in the baptism that Jesus underwent. By this Cullmann does not mean the baptism in the River Jordan but the baptism of suffering on the cross of Calvary. Jesus seems to refer to this coming experience of distress and desolation as a 'baptism' in Mark 10.38–39 and Luke 12.49–51. The former reference is very allusive, but the latter more explicit — 'I have a baptism to undergo, and how distressed I am until it is completed'. The relationship between baptism and death is clearly of great theological significance in the life of Jesus, and in the Christian believer. However, although this is worked out in some detail in Romans 6.1–4 and also mentioned in Colossians 2.12, the death of *Jesus* is nowhere in the New Testament referred to as a baptism — apart from the two implicit (rather than explicit) references in Mark and Luke referred to above. Thus it scarcely

seems the place to *start* to develop a theology of Christian baptism.

5. Another line is to commence with *the command of Jesus* himself in the so-called Great Commission of Matthew 28.19–20, 'Go and make disciples of all nations, baptizing them in the name of the Father and of the Son and of the Holy Spirit, and teaching them to obey everything I have commanded you'. A recent book by Eric Lane[2] asserts that 'these words form the only true basis for the study of Christian baptism'.[3] He goes on to indicate that this clearly implies baptism is for confessing believers only.

There have been lengthy scholarly debates about the authenticity of this passage where the risen Jesus leaves his marching orders with the disciples. These debates are frequently subjective and inconclusive.[4] We can firmly accept the Great Commission as indicating (if not the *ipsissima verba* of the risen Christ) the very early 'conviction that the practice of Christian baptism had the full authority of Jesus behind it'.[5]

While acknowledging the importance of the Lord's authority behind this passage, the significance of the context of evangelism and teaching, and the notable Trinitarian reference, significant features of Christian baptism are unmentioned. There is no reference to forgiveness of sin, the gift of the Holy Spirit, or incorporation into the Church. Important though this passage is, it does not provide the key into the theological significance of Christian baptism.

6. Other writers begin with the baptismal *practice of the early Church* as seen in the Acts of the Apostles. There are nine instances of baptism in this story of early Church growth – the day of Pentecost (2.38–41), in Samaria (8.12–17), the Ethiopian (8.36–38), Saul (9.17–18), Cornelius with relatives and friends (10.47–48; 11.15–18), Lydia and household (16.15), the jailer of Philippi and household (16.31–34), Cris-

pus with his household and others in Corinth (18.8) and the disciples at Ephesus (19.1–7).

Here we find all the distinctive features of Christian baptism:

(a) it is 'in the name of Jesus Christ' implying allegiance to him (e.g. 2.38; 10.48)
(b) it is closely linked to preaching of the gospel and making disciples (in every instance)
(c) it involves repentance and faith and leads to forgiveness of sins (e.g. 2.38; 8.12, etc.)
(d) it usually (though not always) includes the gift of the Holy Spirit (e.g. 2.38; 19.5–6)
(e) it usually implies incorporation into the church (e.g. 2.41).

However, the picture which emerges is not entirely straightforward. Frequently one or several of the five characteristics listed above are omitted, though any argument from silence is of little value. More strange is the baptism by Philip of the believers in Samaria after 'he preached the good news of the kingdom of God, and the name of Jesus Christ' but the Holy Spirit is unmentioned and unreceived. It was some time later that the apostles Peter and John came, and prayed for the Holy Spirit who came through the laying on of their hands. The explanation given is 'that the Holy Spirit had not yet come upon any of them; they had simply been baptized into the name of the Lord Jesus' (verse 16). Here, in only the second recorded instance of baptism in the Early Church, baptism seems strangely downgraded and needing 'confirmation' by apostolic hands for reception of the Spirit. Also remarkable is the experience of Cornelius and company who receive the Holy Spirit *prior* to baptism. Then again the disciples at Ephesus had received only John's baptism and not heard of the Holy Spirit, so after Paul had told them of Jesus, they were (re)baptized into his name and received the Holy Spirit through Paul's laying hands on them.

It may well be argued that the Acts narratives indicate a pattern of baptism in the name of Jesus following preaching of Christ which results in repentance and faith. The relationship of the gift of the Spirit and incorporation into the Church in this process of initiation is, however, not always clear. Were the believers in Samaria who had been 'baptized into Jesus' really members of the body of Christ before they received the Holy Spirit? What is the significance of the 'laying on of hands' in three (Samaria, Saul, Ephesus) of the four occasions when the receiving of the Holy Spirit is clearly spelled out? — and in the fourth (Cornelius), the Holy Spirit precedes baptism.

The whole pattern of initiation events does not always follow a logical and ordered progression. Teaching may be inadequate (as at Ephesus) and God's Spirit is sovereign and free (as in the Cornelius episode) — and so oddities and inconsistencies occur. It will be seen later that various kinds of similar problems arise nowadays. Sufficient at the moment to note that it is not so straightforward as some may suggest simply to say that we should follow the pattern of the Early Church. Furthermore, the narratives in Acts are just that — narratives — and provide no coherent explanation of the significance of baptism. There are a cluster of five features which seem associated with baptismal events (as we noted on p. 15) but we need to look to other parts of Scripture for more systematic and careful teaching of Christian faith and practice.

7. Thus we turn to the *teaching of the Letters*. There is nowhere in the New Testament that baptism receives a systematic treatment. The references in the Letters use baptism as an illustration to develop some other

theme. So the questions we raise about its meaning, who should be baptized, and the manner of baptism may not be dealt with explicitly. However, it is important to study this teaching in some detail.

The teaching of the Letters

There are nine passages in the Letters where baptism is mentioned explicitly and eight other passages where the reference is probable.

1 *Explicit references to Christian baptism*

(i) Romans 6.3–4 in the context of an appeal for Christian holiness —
All of us who were baptized into Christ Jesus were baptized into his death. We were therefore buried with him through baptism into death in order that, just as Christ was raised from the dead through the glory of the Father, we too may live a new life.

(ii) 1 Corinthians 1.13–17 in the context of an appeal for Christian unity —
Is Christ divided? Was Paul crucified for you? Were you baptized into the name of Paul? I am thankful that I did not baptize any of you except Crispus and Gaius, so no one can say that you were baptized into my name. (Yes, I also baptized the household of Stephanas; beyond that I don't remember if I baptized anyone else.) For Christ did not send me to baptize, but to preach the gospel — not with words of human wisdom, lest the cross of Christ be emptied of its power.

(iii) 1 Corinthians 10.1–4 in the context of warnings about discipline in Christian life —
For I do not want you to be ignorant of the fact, brothers, that our forefathers were all under the

cloud and that they all passed through the sea. They were all baptized into Moses in the cloud and in the sea. They all ate the same spiritual food and drank the same spiritual drink; for they drank from the spiritual rock that accompanied them, and that rock was Christ.

(iv) 1 Corinthians 12.13 in the context of an appeal for unity in Christ —
For we were all baptized by one Spirit into one body — whether Jews or Greeks, slave or free — and we were all given the one Spirit to drink.

(v) 1 Corinthians 15.29 in the context of an argument for resurrection of the dead —
Now if there is no resurrection, what will those do who are baptized for the dead? If the dead are not raised at all, why are people baptized for them?

(vi) Galatians 3.26–29 in the context of an argument for Christian unity through faith in Christ Jesus —
You are all sons of God through faith in Christ Jesus, for all of you who were united with Christ in baptism have been clothed with Christ. There is neither Jew nor Greek, slave nor free, male nor female, for you are all one in Christ Jesus. If you belong to Christ, then you are Abraham's seed, and heirs according to the promise.

(vii) Ephesians 4.3–5 in the context of an appeal for Christian unity —
Make every effort to keep the unity of the Spirit through the bond of peace. There is one body and one Spirit — just as you were called to one hope when you were called — one Lord, one faith, one baptism.

(viii) Colossians 2.11–13 in the context of teaching on true freedom in Christ —

In him you were also circumcised, in the putting off of your sinful nature, not with a circumcision done by the hands of men but with the circumcision done by Christ, having been buried with him in baptism and raised with him through your faith in the power of God, who raised him from the dead.

When you were dead in your sins and in the uncircumcision of your sinful nature, God made you alive with Christ.

(ix) 1 Peter 3.18–21 in the context of teaching on the place of suffering in Christian life —

For Christ died for your sins once for all, the righteous for the unrighteous, to bring you to God. He was put to death in the body but made alive by the Spirit, through whom also he went and preached to the spirits in prison who disobeyed long ago when God waited patiently in the days of Noah while the ark was being built. In it only a few people, eight in all, were saved through water, and this water symbolizes baptism that now saves you also — not the removal of dirt from the body but the pledge of a good conscience toward God. It saves you by the resurrection of Jesus Christ.

Two features of the apostolic understanding of baptism clearly emerge — the ethical consequences of baptism and the Old Testament covenant context of baptism.

The *ethical consequences* of baptism are apparent from the fact that four of the passages use baptism as an illustration of the radically new behaviour expected of a believer in Christ. The Romans and Colossians verses speak particularly of baptism as some kind of identification with the death, burial and resurrection of Jesus whereby the old life is dead, and the believer now lives a new life in Christ. Another four passages use baptism as an indication of and argument for the essential unity of all who share faith in the one Christ, and are 'in him'.

The *Old Testament covenant context* of Christian baptism is apparent because in at least four of the passages the writer draws a clear parallel with an Old Testament covenant episode. The remarkable nature and significance of these parallels is not generally understood, and so needs to be unpacked:

1. In Galatians 3.26–29 it is asserted that those who belong to Christ through faith and baptism are '*Abraham's seed*, and heirs according to the promise'. Thus not only are slave/freeman and male/female divisions overcome but also the Jew/Gentile. However, the implication is not that the Jewish people lose their covenant relationship and promise (and become like Gentiles), but that the Gentiles through Christ enter into the covenant relationship and promise (and become 'a chosen people, a royal priesthood, a holy nation, a people belonging to God', 1 Peter 2.9). The covenant with Abraham included the promise of seed and heirs, not according to human design but by the supernatural and spiritual work of God, i.e. not through Ishmael but through Isaac 'the child of promise'. Paul is saying here that this promise to Abraham is fulfilled in Christ and those who are 'baptized in Christ'. An understanding of baptism into Christ involves knowing about God's covenant promises to Abraham, their history and fulfilment.

2. In Colossians 2.11–13 it is asserted that in Christ his people receive *circumcision* understood as a moral and spiritual operation, and that this happened in association with baptism-burial and faith-resurrection. In view of the misuse and misunder-

standing of circumcision that Paul tackles so vigorously in Galatians and Philippians it is all the more remarkable that here he brings so closely together the initiation rites of circumcision and baptism and indicates that they symbolize the same spiritual realities of moral and spiritual transformation — death to a selfish way, new life to a godly way. The implication is not that the Jewish people lose their covenant sign of circumcision (rightly understood) but that the Gentiles through Christ enter into the spiritual realities of the covenant sign of circumcision by means of the new and more widely appropriate rite of baptism. Paul is saying without embarrassment that those baptized in Christ are circumcised spiritually. An understanding then of baptism involves knowing about God's covenant-sign of circumcision, its origin, meaning and use.

3. In 1 Peter 3.18–21 it is asserted that baptism which brings salvation — understood not merely as outward and physical washing but as inward and spiritual renewal — is symbolized in the *water of Noah's flood*, or rather God's flood, through which Noah and his family were kept safe. There are many difficulties in understanding the previous verses, but there can be no doubt that the author draws a clear parallel between the experience of salvation associated with the water of baptism and the salvation through the water of the flood. It may seem a strange comparison to us now, but it obviously had a clear and compelling connection then. An understanding of baptism into Christ will be helped by knowledge of God's salvation of Noah through the flood which is so closely associated with the covenant promise of mercy and the covenant sign in the rainbow.

4. In 1 Corinthians 10.1–4 Paul uses typically New Testament sacramental language about the experi-

ences of *the Israelites journeying with Moses* from Egypt towards the promised land. He describes the passing through the sea and being under the cloud as a 'baptism into Moses in the cloud and in the sea'. Furthermore he describes the divinely provided manna and the water that came out of the rock as 'spiritual food' and 'spiritual drink'. In the context of baptism this appears to be a reference to the eating and drinking of Holy Communion. This interpretation is surely made certain by the following words: 'They drank from the spiritual rock that accompanied them, and that rock was *Christ*'. Just as, in Colossians 2, Paul has no embarrassment about asserting that the same spiritual realities are symbolized in circumcision and baptism, so here he uses baptism to explain the experience of the cloud and the sea, eucharistic language to explain the provision of food and drink, and caps it all by saying that it was Christ who was with them as the Sustainer. Just as Christ and the sacraments he instituted cast light on the Israelites' experience, is it not clear that our understanding of these sacraments will be enlightened by an appreciation of what God was doing with the Israelites and Moses? The journey they were engaged in was clearly because God remembered his covenant with Abraham, with Isaac and with Jacob (Exodus 2.24), redeemed them from slavery and, leading them to a new life, he renews that same covenant. The whole Exodus story refers insistently back to the covenant with Abraham and interprets God's present action as God's faithfulness to and renewal of it. Exodus 6.2–8 should be read carefully, noting the covenant promise of verse 7 'I will take you as my own people, and I will be your God'.

These four references to Abraham's seed, circumcision, Noah and to Moses are quite explicit associations of baptism with Old Testament covenant episodes. As a footnote to this section it may be suggested that a fifth passage, 1 Corinthians 12.13, might be relevant too — 'we were all baptized by one Spirit . . . and were all given the one *Spirit to drink'*. In the light of Paul's references just two chapters earlier to drinking from the spiritual rock which was Christ, and because it is the Spirit of Christ we drink, the connection seems apparent. But even if not, the case is clearly made in the other four passages. When referring to baptism, the apostles moved naturally to the classic covenant-passages of the Old Testament for explanation and illustration.

We now move on in our consideration of the New Testament Epistles to —

2. *Probable references to Christian baptism*

All the following passages are regarded as baptismal by the (Baptist) theologian G. R. Beasley-Murray in his large and detailed study *Baptism in the New Testament*. The evidence for this conclusion is presented there with meticulous care.

Four passages use the metaphor of *washing*. The idea of cleansing from sin is obvious in both the baptism of John and in Christian baptism. The connection is made explicit in Acts 22.16 where Paul in his testimony quotes Ananias as saying to him, 'Get up, be baptized and *wash* your sins away, calling on God's name'.

(i) 1 Corinthians 6.11 in the context of teaching that the wicked will not inherit the kingdom of God —

And that is what some of you were. But you were washed, you were sanctified, you were justified in the name of the Lord Jesus Christ and by the Spirit of our God.

(ii) Ephesians 5.25–27 in the context of Christian relationships between husbands and wives —

Husbands, love your wives, just as Christ loved the church and gave himself up for her to make her holy, cleansing her by the washing with water through the word, and to present her to himself as a radiant church, without stain or wrinkle or any other blemish, but holy and blameless.

(iii) Titus 3.5–7 in the context of the decisively new character of life in Christ —
He saved us through the washing of rebirth and renewal by the Holy Spirit, whom he poured out on us generously through Jesus Christ our Saviour, so that, having been justified by his grace, we might become heirs having the hope of eternal life.

(iv) Hebrews 10.22–23 in the context of a call to perseverance in the new life of Christ —
Let us draw near to God with a sincere heart in full assurance of faith, having our hearts sprinkled to cleanse us from a guilty conscience and having our bodies washed with pure water. Let us hold unswervingly to the hope we profess, for he who promised is faithful.

Three passages use the metaphor of the *seal*. This stamp or mark of God's ownership is the Holy Spirit. Paul uses the same word in Romans 4.11 — Abraham 'received the sign of circumcision, a seal of righteousness'. In the rite of infant circumcision there was a prayer blessing God who 'sealed his offspring with the sign of a holy covenant'.[6] By the second century AD the term 'seal' was used explicitly of Christian baptism. It was, then, commonly used of both rites of initiation — circumcision and baptism. Baptismal ideas are used in each context, so it is widely agreed that these passages refer to baptism. The metaphor of a seal involves an outward sign of an inward reality.

If the inward reality is the gift of the Holy Spirit, surely the outward sign is the mark of baptism. For a contrary interpretation see R. E. O. White.[7]

(v) 2 Corinthians 1.20–22 in the context of the faithfulness of God —
For no matter how many promises God has made, they are 'Yes' in Christ. And so through him the 'Amen' is spoken by us to the glory of God. Now it is God who makes both us and you stand firm in Christ. He anointed us, set his seal of ownership on us, and put his Spirit in our hearts as a deposit, guaranteeing what is to come.

(vi) Ephesians 1.13–14 in the context of God's eternal plan of spiritual blessings in Christ —
And you also were included in Christ when you heard the word of truth, the gospel of your salvation. In him, when you believed, you were marked with a seal, the promised Holy Spirit, who is a deposit guaranteeing our inheritance until the redemption of those who are God's possession — to the praise of his glory.

(vii) Ephesians 4.30 in the context of holy living —
And do not grieve the Holy Spirit of God, with whom you were sealed for the day of redemption.

Three passages use the metaphor of *anointing*. It symbolizes equipment for service and is associated with the outpouring of God's Spirit (1 Samuel 16.13; Isaiah 61.1). The apostle Peter says, 'After the baptism that John preached, God anointed Jesus of Nazareth with the Holy Spirit and power' (Acts 16.37–38). The association of ideas of separation to God and empowering with the Spirit point both to the baptism of Jesus, the Anointed One and to the baptism of his people who became known as Christians, those separated to Christ and, like him, baptized in Spirit.

For the reference in 2 Corinthians 1.20–22 see (v) on p. 26 because it is used with the sealing metaphor.

(viii) 1 John 2.20 and 27 in the context if warnings against false teachings and antichrists —
But you have an anointing from the Holy One, and all of you know the truth.
As for you, the anointing you received from him remains in you, and you do not need anyone to teach you. But as his anointing teaches you about all things and as that anointing is real, not counterfeit — just as it has taught you, remain in him.

Two features of baptism clearly emerge from all these passages — the ethical consequences of baptism and its Old Testament covenant context. The same matters were apparent in the earlier consideration of the explicit references to baptism (see p. 19).

The *ethical consequences* are clearly seen in every passage. They speak of the dramatic action of God whereby a new life begins in Christ and by the Spirit. This life is marked by holiness, purity, perseverance, knowledge of the truth and security until the eventual 'day of redemption'.

The *Old Testament covenant context* is apparent because every passage is full of Old Testament covenant imagery. Of the Hebrews passage Beasley-Murray says with excusable hyperbole 'every syllable is reminiscent of the Old Testament cultus'.[8] There are at least seven categories to notice:

1. *Washing* and cleansing was a prominent feature of the ceremonial system. Priests were washed at their consecration (Exodus 29.4) and Levites sprinkled with water (Numbers 8.7). Special washings were required of the chief priest on the Day of Atonement

(Leviticus 16.4,24,26) and by anyone who was defiled with impurity (Leviticus 11.40; 15.5ff; 17.15; 22.6; Deuteronomy 23.11). The large bronze basin between the tent and the altar was a constant indication of the need for cleansing and purity in the worship and service of God (Exodus 30.17–21). This great emphasis on washing and cleansing was a constant reminder of the holiness of the God who established the covenant, and his gracious means for his redeemed people to maintain their response to the covenant in holy separation to God.

2. *Sealing* was a widely known custom throughout the ancient Near East. Many thousands of individual engraved seals have been discovered. The use of a seal marks ownership and implies security, and the term is used both literally and metaphorically in the Old Testament. Paul's description of circumcision as both a sign and seal to Abraham (Romans 4.11) gives insight into how the covenant-sign was understood. It was a mark of God's ownership and a pledge of God's faithfulness — in the context of God's everlasting covenant (see Genesis 15, especially vv. 2, 7, 9–11, 13).

3. *Anointing* was frequently performed in Old Testament times on persons and things to signify holiness, i.e. separation unto God. Kings, priests and prophets were anointed with oil. It was essentially an act of God's authority — as when Samuel poured oil on Saul's head saying 'Has not the Lord anointed you leader over his inheritance?' (1 Samuel 10.1), and is profoundly solemn. As noted earlier, it symbolized equipment for service through the outpouring of God's Spirit (1 Samuel 16.13; Isaiah 61.1). The Hebrew word 'messiah' and Greek equivalent 'christ' mean 'the anointed'. The special task of anointed leaders was to help the people in maintaining the

covenant. The Anointed One (Messiah, Christ) would perform this uniquely.

4. The idea of *promise* occurs three times. In 2 Corinthians 1 'God's promises', in Ephesians 1 'the Holy Spirit of promise', in Hebrews 10 'God promised'. The history of God's salvation (i.e. biblical theology) is a great pattern of promise and fulfilment with lines from Abraham, Moses, David and the prophets converging on Christ. This is the everlasting covenant by which God makes himself a people (see Jeremiah 31, Joel 2.28).

5. The language of *inheritance* occurs twice as does also the closely associated idea of *hope*. In Ephesians 1 'our inheritance', in Titus 3 'heirs having the hope', and in Hebrews 10 'the hope we profess'. Inheritance is rich with covenant associations. Canaan was God's inheritance (Exodus 15.17; Psalm 79.1) but promised to Abraham (Genesis 12.7; 13.15; 15.18–21 etc.). Spiritually God was to be the inheritance of Israel (Psalm 16.5–6) just as Israel was to be God's (Deuteronomy 7.6; 32.9). The New Testament picks up this concept, and expresses the hope that in Christ his people are heirs of God, heirs according to promise, inheritors of the kingdom of God (Romans 8.17; Galatians 3.29; Matthew 25.34).

6. *Redemption* occurs twice in Ephesians 1 and 4. In both cases the Holy Spirit seals or guarantees believers or their inheritance until the final day of redemption. Redemption is used of God's deliverance of the Israelites from Egypt (Exodus 6.6; Psalm 77.15) but this looked forward to a freedom that was not fully realized until Christ's redemption on the cross, and even that is not fully consummated until his triumphant return. Till then the Holy Spirit is the guarantee. God's covenant is with his redeemed people and until the day of redemption.

7. The *bridegroom-bride* imagery of God and his people in Ephesians 5 comes from the Old Testament covenant promises too (Isaiah 54.6; Jeremiah 2.2; 3.20; Ezekiel 16.8; Hosea 2.16).

The Old Testament covenant imagery is overwhelmingly apparent in all these passages that probably or possibly refer to baptism, just as they were in key passages that spoke explicitly of baptism. This is a matter of cardinal importance because it clearly indicates that baptism is understood by the letter writers against this background, and furthermore, this background is not just incidental to understanding baptism — it is *the* theological context.

The case is clearly made in these pastoral-teaching letters, but when we look back to other references to baptism in the Gospels and Acts we find the same two features of ethical consequences and covenant language. In John's ministry of baptism there is the call to genuine moral repentance, and this is to prepare the way for covenant renewal in the kingdom-reign of God through the Messiah. Just as proselytes were baptized to become 'children of the covenant' John urges the same upon Jews — with a view to covenant-faithfulness.

Jesus' baptism was to fulfill all righteousness i.e. to do what God required. It was also his commitment to sacrificial death for sinners, the baptism of Calvary, which would establish 'the new covenant in my blood' as he said at the Last Supper (Luke 22.20).

The Great *Commission* includes teaching obedience to everything Jesus commanded and also the typically covenant promise 'I will be with you always'.

In the *Acts* baptism is obviously linked with repentance, forgiveness and new life — the washing away of sins (22.16) but also the covenant promise is explicitly there in 1.4 and 2.39.

Where shall we start? Back on p. 11 we noted the procedural dilemma over whether to start in the Old Testament or in the New. It has now become clear that a consideration of the New Testament references drives us back to the Old Testament to understand the nature of God's covenant. The reason for this is entirely biblical. It is not in order to justify infant baptism (through comparison with circumcision) as argued by Lane[9] and many other baptist writers. He says 'If there had been no argument over the baptizing of infants, it is doubtful whether Genesis 17 and the covenant of circumcision would ever have entered into the matter. The appeal to it was made, not to teach the *nature and meaning* of baptism itself, but to justify a certain *way of practising it*' (his italics). This is a tragic misunderstanding. It is the New Testament itself which sends us back to the Old Testament covenant situations to understand the nature and meaning of baptism. If we are to be biblical we can do no other! The argument for or against infant baptism should not be allowed to interfere with following where the evidence requires. If the covenant context was vital to the apostles, it is of crucial theological import to us too — whatever our convictions about infant baptism.

It is a major weakness of the report *Baptism, Eucharist and Ministry* that in its Baptism statement it makes no reference at all to this covenant context. It speaks of baptism as 'entry into the New Covenant', and refers to 'symbolic uses of water in the Old Testament', 'salvation from the flood' and 'an exodus from bondage' but nowhere are these images linked by the covenant theme. This leads to serious problems later when the statement addresses issues of practice – as we shall see (p. 103).

3
God's Covenant

The Bible is a whole library of books, a vast canvas of history, law, prophecy, poetry, proverb, gospel, epistle and apocalyptic. It is all too easy to miss the wood for the trees. Is there a central theme, a golden thread running throughout? Yes — and it is quite simply this — God wanted a people for himself, children, friends, a family.

God created human beings 'in his image' for this very purpose. God made loving provision for human need, offered loving fellowship and looked for loving response. But humanity refused the constraints of love, asserted a unilateral declaration of independence and rebelled against the expression of God's nature i.e. his holy will. The result was (and is) inevitable and devastating. Humanity is cut off from God, and under his judgement. There are two aspects to this judgement — it is both an expression of the holiness of God (who cannot look upon sin), and an expression of the love of God (who does not just leave the situation like that).

The covenant story

God's love for humanity and longing for a people involved a plan of rescue, salvation. This was entirely God's initiative which is what the word 'grace' means in the Bible. The rescue plan involved atonement for sin (i.e. action to undo its consequences), forgiveness for the rebels, and reconciliation into friendship and a new way of life. This plan of salvation is frequently summarized by God as 'I will be your God, and you will be my people'. God does not force this rescue-plan on humanity, for there cannot be compulsion to receive or offer love. Rather God offers the plan as a gift – and that is summed up in the biblical word 'covenant'. This covenant is not an agreement between equals, but is an agreement devised and offered by the mighty, holy and yet merciful God to people who are spiritually in exile, helpless and bankrupt. The basis of the salvation must therefore be provided entirely by God and his grace. All that human beings can do is to accept God's plan and offer, to believe his promise and receive his gift — and that is what the Bible means by 'faith'. Doing good things (good works) could never undo the basic rebellion, or offer any basis for humanity deserving God's forgiveness and friendship. God's covenant plan of salvation can be summed up by the two words — *grace* (from God) and *faith* (by which the salvation is accepted).

But how did God effect this atonement, this forgiveness and this reconciliation. He did it, not by overlooking the rebellion and iniquity, but in an amazing and supremely costly way by taking the judgement on himself! 'God was in Christ reconciling the world to himself' (2 Corinthians 5.19) and 'Christ himself bore our sins in his body on the tree' (1 Peter 2.24). The whole plan is centred on Jesus Christ, God's Son and his death on the cross.

So from our vantage point in history we can see that the story of God's covenant plan of salvation falls into two phases, BC and AD. Before Christ, the people of the covenant were looking forward through pictures, types and shadows for the fulfilment of the covenant promises. The coming of Christ ushers in the new era — through his death and resurrection and gift of the Spirit. The first phase is characterized by 'promise'; the second phase is marked by 'fulfilment'.

The Greek word for 'covenant' in the Bible also

means testament (i.e. will) and was translated into the Latin 'testamentum' — hence the accepted name for the two sections of the Bible as testaments. The idea of an old and new testament/covenant comes from 2 Corinthians 3 verses 14 and 6. In the Old Testament the covenant was offered in an imperfect, temporary and provisional way (the 'old'), but when Christ came, the covenant was revealed in its perfect, permanent and eternal glory (the 'new' covenant). Thus, as we shall now see from a detailed look at the biblical development of the theme, there is throughout the Bible —

> One Lord — Yahweh is the God and Father of our Lord Jesus Christ
> One plan of salvation — 'I will be your God and you will be my people'
> One basis of atonement — the sacrificial death of Jesus Christ
> One way to receive salvation — by faith in God's promises
> One covenant of grace — planned in eternity and worked out in history

We have seen in chapter 2 that the Old Testament covenant context is *the* theological context for understanding baptism into Christ. We shall now find that this covenant idea is the central theme of the Old Testament and absolutely fundamental to its religious teaching. In this summary of the covenant story, we have the advantage of retrospect, of looking at the 'old' through the light of the 'new'. As Augustine said:

> the new is in the old concealed
> the old is in the new revealed.

But we shall now examine the development of the covenant concept historically in order to understand it in its own (Old Testament) terms, and not just through Christian (New Testament) spectacles.

The background to the idea of covenant (Hebrew, berith) in the Old Testament is to be found in ancient Near Eastern peace treaties between kings and between nations. These are well known from the third millennium B.C. In a friendly relationship between conqueror and vassal the language of 'father and son' was used. In a more stern relationship it was 'lord and servant'. The idea of a covenant relationship between a god and a king or his people was also widespread.[1]

Covenant introduced — Noah

It is in the story of Noah in Genesis 6–9 that the word 'covenant' first occurs in the Bible. When God saw the depravity that resulted from human rebellion against his love and his law, he 'was grieved that he had made man on the earth, and his heart was filled with pain' (6.6). God decided on annihilation as the just course of action, but 'Noah found favour in the eyes of the Lord' (6.8). This means that God's grace found Noah — and as a result of God's love in his life he is described as 'righteous' (6.9) because he 'walked with God' i.e. lived God's way. God determined to save Noah, told him to build the ark, and explains 'I will establish my covenant with you' (6.18).

Certain characteristics of this covenant are clear: (a) It was God's initiative of grace. (b) There is a 'family principle'. (c) Noah and his family had the obligation of obedience in order to enjoy the covenant — they had to build the ark and enter it. (d) Later, after the flood was over, Noah showed his gratitude by means of worship and sacrifice (8.20).

After this, God extended the covenant of physical security to the whole of humanity by promising never again to destroy the earth (9.6). The characteristics of this covenant are: (a) Once again it is a sovereign act of God's grace — '*I* will establish *my* covenant'. (b) the covenant is not just with Noah and his family, but for all humanity. (c) There are no conditions attached and so the covenant cannot be broken formally. However, there is in the context an implicit obligation of gratitude for the covenant faithfulness of regular seasons and harvest. (d) The covenant is everlasting. (e) God gives a 'sign of the covenant' — the rainbow. Remarkably, God says 'Whenever the rainbow appears in the clouds, *I* will see and remember the everlasting covenant' (9.16). The sign was a pledge of *God's* faithfulness, of God's memory. The sign expresses God's promises, and invites the response of trust.

This story is used as an illustration of the significance of baptism in 1 Peter 3.18–22 (as we saw on p. 19).

Although this story contains the first explicit reference to God's covenant, there is the earlier clue to God's intention of rescue in Genesis 3.15 when God curses the serpent-tempter and says that his head will be crushed by a descendant of the woman.

Covenant clarified — Abraham

In the Abraham stories of Genesis 12–24, the covenant-principle is filled out and clarified in a striking and exemplary pattern. This covenant, with its remarkable promises, is proposed with a divine call in chapter 12, developed with divine sacrifice in chapter 15, and confirmed with a divine sign in chapter 17.

In chapter 12 the word covenant does not appear, but the promises are clearly made: (a) the *spiritual* promise that God is adopting Abraham and his family for blessing (v.1–3); (b) the *national* promise of a great nation and name (v.2); (c) the *universal* promise that 'all peoples on earth will be blessed through you' (v.3);

(d) the *territorial* promise is hinted at in verse 1 and clarified in verse 7. Abraham's response was clearly to believe God's promises, and to act on the basis of them — he left his country to travel with God, and frequently he worships the Lord, by building an altar and calling on the Lord's name.

In chapter 15 the Lord clarifies the covenant (v.18) and develops three of the promises: (a) the *spiritual* promise of mutual relationship in verse 1 'I am your shield, your very great reward'; (b) the *national* promise of a real son, and great family (v.4f); (c) the *territorial* promise of the land (v.7,18). God confirms the promise through sacrifice, (v.9–18). The symbolism is that as God's presence in the smoking fire pot and blazing torch passes between the pieces of the sacrifice, God takes a vivid and terrible oath 'so may it be to me if this oath is broken' (see Jeremiah 34.18 and 1 Samuel 11.7). In that day of sacrifice, the Lord made a covenant, and in the oath took upon himself the obligation of the covenant — even if broken! Abraham's response is faith in God's promise, 'Abraham believed the Lord, and he credited it to him as righteousness' (v.6), — and obedience, in providing the elements for sacrifice.

Abraham was not always trusting and obedient. The story is riveting as he twists and turns to manage things in a human way, while God patiently bides his time to teach Abraham that there is a better way of covenant promise.

Thus in chapter 17 God confirms the promises with a covenant-sign. The promises are again: (i) *spiritual* — 'I will be your God . . . walk before me and be blameless' (v.1,7); (ii) *national* — the promise of many nations and kings indicates more than a narrow nationalism (v.4–6); (iii) *territorial* — the land (v.7).

The confirming covenant-sign is *circumcision* (v.9–14). The cutting off of a small piece of the loose foreskin of the male sex organ was a common practice in the ancient Near East but was usually associated with puberty, coming of age and sexual maturity. God, as so often, takes a common ritual or symbol and invests it with an entirely new significance. It becomes a mark of God's ownership, God's promises and God's covenant — not a mark any longer of human achievement or maturity, but of God's initiative and grace. Incidentally, it spoke of the God-given sacredness of sex in a sexually decadent society. Though performed only on the male, the mark and its symbolism would be constantly shared with his wife, and would be (as we might say) at the heart of every act of love and procreation.

It cannot be too strongly emphasized that God's covenant of circumcision was never meant to be merely an outward sign of natural birth or racial descent. From the beginning it is a mark of God's ownership, of God's covenant promise and blessing — of God's offer of communion and friendship. It was, therefore, an outward and physical sign of something inward and spiritual. This is so widely misunderstood that some of the evidence must be set out fully. Because of God's electing love, he expects fearful obedience and loving service, so 'circumcise your hearts, and do not be stiff-necked' (Deuteronomy 10.12–16). The Lord your God will circumcise your hearts and the hearts of your descendants, so that you may love him with all your heart and with all your soul, and live' (Deuteronomy 30.6). 'If they will confess their sins — their treachery and hostility towards me . . . then when their uncircumcised hearts are humbled . . . I will remember my covenant' (Leviticus 26.40–42).

The prophet Jeremiah understood it in the same way as a mark of God's holy covenant which separates people to God and thus calls for the response of a separated, holy life. 'Circumcise yourselves to the Lord, circumcise your hearts' (4.4). 'Who will listen to me? Their ears are closed (literally, in the Hebrew, uncircumcised) so that they cannot hear' (6.10). The Lord says, 'I will punish all who are circumcised only in the flesh . . . all these nations are really uncircumcised, and even the whole house of Israel is uncircumcised in heart' (9.25–26). The physical and spiritual aspects of new life are to be essentially related in the covenant.

Once again Abraham's response is trustful worship (17.3) and obedient keeping of the covenant (v.9–14).

The characteristics of this clarified covenant with Abraham can be summarized: (a) it is by God's initiative of grace — and includes promises both spiritual and territorial; (b) there is a God-given covenant-sign which seals God's ownership and motivates response; (c) there is a family-principle, including not only infants but all within the household (17.12–13); (d) there is a clear obligation of personal faith and obedience, and the directing of children and household 'to keep the way of the Lord by doing what is right and just' (18.19), i.e. there is a conditional element, and the covenant blessings are not automatic either on the basis of birth or of the sign; (e) it is an everlasting covenant (17.7,13).

This covenant with Abraham is referred to frequently in the later salvation-history of the Scriptures — it is of seminal significance! It is to be noted that the covenant is:

spiritual — not only material and physical
eternal — not only temporal
universal — not only national
conditional — not automatic

Covenant developed — Moses

Later the Israelite tribes became slaves in Egypt, and their cry for help was heard by God. The story is in the book Exodus. 'God heard their groaning and he remembered his covenant with Abraham, with Isaac and with Jacob' (2.24). God met with Moses and explained his plan of rescue. He repeatedly describes himself as the God of Abraham i.e. the covenant God. God tells Moses 'I am the Lord. I appeared to Abraham, to Isaac and to Jacob . . . I also established my covenant with them . . . and I have remembered my covenant . . . I will free you . . . and redeem you . . . I will take you as my own people, and I will be your God' (6.2–8).

After the great escape, God told Moses on Mount Sinai what he was to say to the people, 'You yourselves have seen what I did to Egypt, and how I carried you on eagles' wings and brought you to myself. Now if you obey me fully and keep my *covenant*, then out of all nations you will be my treasured possession. Although the whole earth is mine, you will be for me a kingdom of priests and a holy nation' (19.4–6). The people said they would accept the covenant, and so they washed their clothes, were consecrated and were led out of the camp to the foot of Mount Sinai 'to meet with God'. The Lord appeared in fire and smoke, and then to Moses revealed his covenant-law in the Ten Commandments and the Book of the Covenant (ch.20–23). The Law was covenant-law because the commandments were prefaced by the covenant-promise 'I am the Lord your God' and a reminder of God's covenant-faithfulness 'who brought you out of Egypt, out of the land of slavery' (20.2).

The covenant was then confirmed with sacrifice, and Moses took some of the blood, sprinkled it on the people, and said, 'This is the blood of the covenant that the Lord has made with you' (24.8). Then follow the instructions for worship and sacrifice — the means of maintaining covenant fellowship and purity. The book Deuteronomy reiterates the electing love of Yahweh, his faithfulness to the covenant and the consequent holiness of the people (Deuteronomy 4.37; 7.6–8; 14.2). This uniquely special relationship is expressed in the intimate terms of parent and child. The Lord says, 'Israel is my firstborn son' (Exodus 4.22) and 'You are the children of the Lord your God' (Deuteronomy 14.1).

The response of the people was expected to be trust in God's promises and obedience to God's laws, but very quickly they found themselves unable to be faithful in these respects. The law and sacrifice were part of God's covenant love. The law is God's way of holy living for redeemed and adopted people of the covenant. Sacrifice is God's way of enabling penitence and forgiveness to those who transgress the covenant.

We may summarize the characteristics of this covenant: (a) it is a development of the covenant with Abraham; (b) by God's initiative of electing love the people are rescued from slavery; (c) the covenant promise is for a spiritual relationship as well as a land; (d) there is an obligation of trust and obedience i.e. faithfulness.

There is a common understanding that this covenant through Moses was a covenant of law (as opposed to grace), and was therefore conditional on human good works (as opposed to faith). This was the way it was often understood by the Israelites themselves — but it is a misunderstanding. We have already seen that the covenant with Abraham was a covenant of grace to be met by faith issuing in obedience. So here too through Moses is a covenant arising out of an act of gracious rescue to be met by faith and obedience. To have the Lord as God, and to be his people, his precious possession, inevitably involves holiness, separation to him. Enjoyment of fellowship with God involves loving him with all one's heart, soul and strength (Deuteronomy 6). 'Be holy, because

I am holy' says the Lord (Leviticus 11.45; 20.26). This should not be understood as legalism — but as filial gratitude.

Covenant preserved — David

The interpretation of the institution of monarchy in the life of Israel has been beset with controversy. Many scholars argue that there are two contradictory accounts. The first in 1 Samuel 9.1–10.16 suggests it was by command of Yahweh with the prophet Samuel's full support; the second in chapter 8 and 10.17–27 suggests there was popular pressure for a king, which was resisted by Samuel and not God's will. The problems with this latter view are that there is no evidence from its inception of opposition to the monarchy in principle (though many of the kings were criticized), it is not easy to disentangle the two accounts, and theocracy (rule of God) is not, in principle, opposed to human leadership, for God can exercise his rule through human leaders as with Moses and the judges.

It is clear that there was grave dissatisfaction religiously, morally and politically, and it seems that God showed his covenant mercy in the institution of the monarchy. Samuel says to Saul 'Has not the Lord anointed you leader over his inheritance?' (1 Samuel 10.1). The Spirit of the Lord comes upon Saul, he prophesies, he is changed into a different person and God is with him (10.6,7). The task of the king is to lead the people in God's way i.e. to maintain the covenant. It is a spiritual responsibility involving a special relationship with God and the anointing of spiritual power.

After Saul's failure, the Lord had said to David 'You shall shepherd my people Israel, and you shall become their ruler' (2 Samuel 5.2). The pattern and character of this new development is clearly seen in 2

Samuel 7 where the Lord announces an everlasting covenant to David. David thought to build God a house, a central place of worship, but God says that he will do something more significant in building a house for David! The covenant promises included a great name, a territory for the people and a dynasty and kingdom that will be everlasting. The covenant refers back to God's gracious redemption from Egypt (v.23), reiterates the relationship that Israel belongs to God, and the Lord is their God (v.24). It uses the intimate language of father and son, and, while promising punishment for wrong, pledges that such chastening will be in the context of unceasing and faithful love (v.14–15). This covenant is celebrated in Psalm 89 especially verses 1–4 and 26–37, and Psalm 132.11–18. 'I have made a covenant with my chosen one, I have sworn to David my servant . . . I will not violate my covenant or alter what my lips have uttered.'

The characteristics of this covenant are: (a) it is God's gracious renewal of his former covenant mercy and promises; (b) it involves intimate spiritual relationship as well as promise of territory; (c) it involves the obligation on the king of living by the Spirit of God, and preserving the rule and law of God as the pattern for the life of his people; (d) it is an everlasting covenant.

The king's task as 'son of God' is to be the 'servant of Yahweh'. He must be the example and enabler to the people of preserving the covenant.

Covenant broken and renewed — the prophets

Repeatedly, the king failed, and the people failed, to keep the covenant. There were notable attempts at renewal which indicate the faithfulness of God's mercy — see Jehoiada and Joash (2 Kings 11.17), and Josiah (2 Kings 23.3). The essential ministry of the prophets was to recall the people to the covenant. The judgement they declared was part of God's mercy. 'The people have broken my covenant and rebelled against my law' (Hosea 8.1; cf. Jeremiah 11.6–10). God's punishment is of a special quality to those who have been chosen, loved and redeemed (Amos 3.2). It is with the purpose of repentance and renewal of the covenant (Hosea 2; Jeremiah 7; Nehemiah 8–10).

The preaching of the prophets was profoundly spiritual and moral — 'I will betroth you in righteousness and justice, in love and compassion. I will betroth you in faithfulness, and you will acknowledge the Lord' (Hosea 2.19–20; cf. Isaiah 61.8–9). Because of continual failure the prophets increasingly looked forward to a new era and a new covenant — yet it was not really a different covenant from God's point of view; the difference and the newness is in the hope that the covenant will be kept and not broken. The idea of universal blessing (promised in the covenant with Abraham) comes through again in the prophets (Isaiah 2.3 and especially 56.3–8). Foreigners are welcome to join God's people and hold fast to his covenant (so also Micah 4.2).

The new era is focussed on a Servant of the Lord who will embody the covenant. Concerning him, God says 'I will make you to be a covenant for the people and a light for the Gentiles' (Isaiah 42.1,6 — also 49.8; 55.3). Jeremiah gives classic expression to this hope of a 'new covenant'. But the difference from the covenant after the Exodus is because the people broke that, though God 'was a husband to them'. Paradoxically, the terms of the new covenant are the same as the old: (a) a spiritual relationship between God and his people; (b) forgiveness of sins; (c) a spiritual response of trusting obedience (Jeremiah 31.31–34; also 32.40; Ezekiel 16.59–63; 37.26–28). These were the very characteristics of the covenant established with

Abraham, and developed with Moses and David. The forgiveness of sins was very clearly implied in God's provision for atonement and sacrifice after the Exodus, while David clearly understood that God's nature is always to have mercy so he blots out transgression, washes away iniquity and cleanses from sin (e.g. Psalm 51).

The Old Testament concludes with the divine promise 'I will send my messenger, who will prepare the way before me. Then suddenly the Lord you are seeking will come to his temple; the messenger of the *covenant*, whom you desire, will come' (Malachi 3.1).

Covenant fulfilled — the Messiah

John the baptizer recalls the people to the covenant terms of sincere repentance, moral cleansing and the reign of God. However, as the last prophet of the old era he points to the Coming One who will baptize with the Holy Spirit and with fire.

Jesus does not use the word 'covenant' frequently, but Zechariah was quite clear that in the birth of John, the forerunner of the Messiah, God was remembering his holy covenant with Abraham (Luke 1.68–79). The whole ministry of Jesus, however, was a demonstration of God's covenant-love. The kingdom-reign of God is breaking in through miracles and signs of salvation; the parables of the kingdom proclaim the grace of God; the teaching of Jesus is that God is to be known intimately as Abba, father, but he requires a discipleship of trust and commitment that is total. This is just like the covenants in the Old Testament.

It is in the evening of the day before he died, in the context of the covenant-Passover meal that Jesus suddenly speaks of his role with breath-taking clarity 'This is my blood of the (new) covenant which is poured out for many for the forgiveness of sins' (Matthew 26.28; Mark 14.24; Luke 22.20; 1 Corinthians

11.25). Thus Jesus makes explicit reference to Moses at Sinai 'This is the blood of the covenant', and the 'new covenant' looked for by Jeremiah (Exodus 24.8; Jeremiah 31.31).

The New Testament writers unite in interpreting the ministry of Jesus in covenant terms — the covenant fulfilled. It seems overwhelmingly clear that the new covenant is strikingly similar to, and continuous with, the old. The supreme benefits are an intimate relationship between God and his people through election, redemption and adoption on the basis of God's grace alone. The conditions are that this offer be trustingly accepted and then worked out in filial gratitude and life with God. In the previous chapter the striking parallels between baptism into Christ and the Old Testament covenant situations were noted — with respect to Noah, to Abraham and circumcision, and to Moses, and the parallel use in the New Testament of Old Testament covenant imagery of washing, sealing, anointing, promise, inheritance (hope), redemption and the marriage-metaphor. The weight of New Testament evidence is enormous, and only a few further examples are noted here. Christ is the Passover (1 Corinthians 5.7), and all God's promises are given their 'Yes' (i.e. their fulfilment) in Christ, (2 Corinthians 1.20). Peter tells the people they are 'heirs of the covenant', and Paul says Christ confirmed the promises to the patriarchs (Acts 3.25; Romans 15.8). The Romans 11 picture of the cultivated olive tree incorporates believing Jews and believing Gentiles sharing together the covenant mercy and purposes of God.

However, there are passages that speak of striking contrasts and discontinuity between the old and new covenants, and they must be carefully studied and understood now:

(a) 2 *Corinthians 3* says the old covenant is of the letter (of the law) and brings condemnation and death, but the new covenant is of the Spirit and brings righteousness and life. But Paul is not speaking here of the electing, redeeming covenant of grace whereby God promised his continuing presence and forgiveness to those who trusted and followed him. We find what Paul means in v.14ff. Those who did not turn to the Lord (in a spiritual conversion) had dull minds and veiled hearts when the old covenant was read, and so God's law simply condemned their self-centred way of life. But where they did turn to the Lord, the law fulfilled its primary purpose of showing God's people his holy will and the way to live in covenant-fellowship with God and others. Similarly since Christ, the Holy Spirit is turning people to God so that they may live.

(b) *Hebrews 8–11* is a sustained exposition of the superiority of the new covenant over the old. The old is obsolete, earthly and involves shadows and copies of reality. The new is a living way, heavenly and involves spiritual realities and better promises. The writer is not suggesting that, before Christ came, God's grace was ineffective and no one really knew and trusted God. The whole of chapter 11 is a catalogue of Old Testament saints who lived by faith in God and were commended for it. 'They did not receive the things promised; they only saw them and welcomed them from a distance . . . they were longing for a better country — a heavenly one. Therefore God is not ashamed to be called their God' (v.13,16). They lived with shadows, copies and promises, while since Christ the realities and the fulfilment can be known. That is one reason for the superiority of the new covenant in Christ. The other reason is the same that Paul spoke of in the previous passage. God found fault with the people who were so frequently unfaithful to the covenant, and promised that by forgiveness and the Holy Spirit's work his people would be more faithful. The blessings and conditions of the covenant are not changed, but fulfilment transcends promise and, it is hoped, spiritual faithfulness will replace widespread unfaithfulness amongst the people of the covenant.

(c) *Romans 9.30–33* contrasts a righteousness through faith in God's salvation and attempts at righteousness through good deeds according to the law. This second course was never what God intended, but many of the Israelites (and, we might add, other religious folk nowadays) misunderstood the covenant through pride, self-sufficiency and not listening to God's word. They replaced grace by law and faith by works. The stumbling-stone then (as now) is the God who invites his people to *trust* him (cf. Isaiah 8.14; 28.16).

(d) *The letter to the Galatians* similarly is a sustained and passionate argument and appeal to Christians who are in grave danger of leaving faith as the basis of their response to God's love in favour of human effort through observance of legal ceremonies and statutes. But those who treat circumcision and the law in this way are 'cursed' because they can never keep it fully and so are condemned to death (chapter 3). In the allegory at the end of chapter 4 Paul contrasts that wrong view of the law of Sinai which leads to spiritual slavery (and which Jerusalem at that time represented) with the covenant through Sarah's child of 'promise' which leads to spiritual liberty with God in the heavenly Jerusalem of the kingdom of God. One symbolizes ordinary human effort, the other represents the work of God's Spirit by promise. In chapter 5 he argues that to submit to the covenant-sign of circumcision as a legal requirement will involve an obligation to the entire ceremonial-legal system, and those who try to be justified by this law-route are separated from the rescue of Christ and grace. And yet, he goes on to explain that those who live by faith in Christ must observe the law rightly understood as genuine love and life according to the Spirit of holiness.

The new covenant is new because after centuries of 'promise', there is now 'fulfilment' through the unfolding of the mystery of Christ (Ephesians 3.1–13). (This is the clue to understanding how even the least in the kingdom of God is greater than John, Matthew 11.11). It is also new because through the clear assurance of forgiveness and baptism of the Spirit there is hope of greater faithfulness in the covenant people of God. But the benefits of the eternal covenant remain the same — an intimate relationship with God; also, its sole basis in the unconditional initiative of God's grace, and the sole means of response in trusting faith issuing in loving obedience. The law does not set aside the promises of grace to Abraham. The law was not given as another route to salvation; it was given to stimulate people to look to the promise of God and faith in him (Galatians 3).

Discontinuities there certainly are, but we are encouraged to remember there is *one* Bible with the two testaments, and we should not insist on a full stop where God only intended a comma. To suggest, as does Beasley-Murray,[2] that the covenants before and after Christ represent death v. life, condemnation v. righteousness and flesh v. spirit is seriously to misconceive the relation of Old and New Testaments and the relation of God's covenant intention of 'grace' to human perversion of it into 'works'. To assert, as he again does,[3] that circumcision had no relation to moral renewal, can only be explained by a phobia of some possible inference of infant baptism rather than a consideration of the actual evidence. Any simplistic contrasts between Old and New Testament in terms of

carnal v. spiritual
national v. universal
letter v. Spirit
law v. grace

are seriously misleading. Promise and fulfilment is the best contrast because it expresses the covenant situation. However, even after the death and resurrection of Jesus Christ and the outpouring of the Spirit at Pentecost, there is yet unfulfilled promise:

Covenant consummated — heaven

'We who have the firstfruits of the Spirit . . . wait eagerly for our adoption as sons, the redemption of our bodies. For in this hope we were saved' (Romans 8.23f; cf. 2 Corinthians 5.1–10). The Holy Spirit of God in our present experience is a wonderful and dramatic fulfilment of Old Testament promise, and yet is a deposit, a down-payment, a guarantee of what is to come. (The Greek word arrabōn is used today of an engagement ring.) The full consummation is to come, and the vision of covenant consummated in heaven is found in Revelation 21. Here is the consummation of the covenant promise to Abraham 'God will live with them' — He will be their God and they will be his people, his children (v.3, 7). Note the covenant imagery of the Holy City, Jerusalem (v.2, 10), marriage (v.2, 4), the life-giving water (v.6), the tribes of Israel (v.12), the temple (v.22), and the repeated emphasis on all the nations sharing in God's final family (v.24f). Finally, as throughout, God's purpose of a response of trusting obedience will also be fulfilled 'Nothing impure will ever enter it . . . but only those whose names are written in the Lamb's book of life' (v.27). God's great covenant of loving, saving compassion is brought to fruition — as he welcomes home his bride!

God's great rescue-plan of salvation, his covenant of grace is centred on his Son, Jesus Christ. While the two phases, BC and AD, differ between promise and fulfilment, the spiritual benefits (of God's grace) and the conditions (of faith leading to holiness) are identical. So Jesus said 'Abraham rejoiced at the thought of seeing my day; he saw it and was glad' (John 8.56), and Paul said 'The Scripture . . . announced the gospel in advance to Abraham: "All nations will be blessed through you"'. (Galatians 3.8)

This is the context in which the New Testament writers understood the nature and meaning of Christian baptism.

4

John and baptism

An important background to Christian baptism is obviously the ministry of John the baptizer. Furthermore John's use of water to symbolize washing has its own antecedents. Before we study those, what about the word itself?

The meaning of the word

The meaning of any word is determined not only by its derivation but, more significantly, by its actual usage within a particular context. Complex discussion about, and examples of, the use of the word in classical and secular Greek, or in the Greek Old Testament, are not actually very helpful. We shall look at how it is used in the New Testament.

The verb baptizō is used in three ways[1]:

(a) of Jewish ritual washing (also the noun, baptismos). E.g. in Mark 7.4 the verb and noun occur, also Luke 11.38 and Hebrews 9.10.
(b) of the religious ceremony of washing with water (also the noun, baptisma), performed by John, by Jesus' disciples during his ministry, and by the early church.
(c) figuratively, e.g. into Moses and in the Holy Spirit (and fire). Also (with the noun, baptisma) of martyrdom (Mark 10.38; Luke 12.50.)

It may mean to dip, or to use water with some special effect, or (metaphorically) to be overwhelmed. The usage of the word does not offer a conclusive answer to the question of the manner of baptism, whether dipping, pouring or sprinkling.[2] Dipping may be appropriate to the imagery of burial, pouring to the imagery of washing or being overwhelmed with the Spirit, while sprinkling with water or with the blood of the covenant was used of consecration in the Old Testament, and may be appropriate to the imagery of anointing or sealing.

The question of the mode of baptism is not settled by the use of the words 'to go down into' and 'to come up out of'. Although this may indicate an immersion, it could just as well indicate going into a river or lake prior to the minister scooping up water to pour it over the candidate's head, i.e. affusion.

Washing with water in the Old Testament

The covenant law of God required frequent washing with water for religious purity, as we have already noted on p. 26. When the prophets pleaded for a moral cleansing in the heart, they were expounding what was always the intention of the ceremonial system in Israel — 'Be holy for I am holy' says the Lord. Isaiah preached 'Wash and make yourselves clean. Take your evil deeds out of my sight! Stop doing wrong, learn to do right' (1.16). Ezekiel 36.25 and Zechariah 13.1 have a similar message. The psalmist, too, prays, 'Cleanse me with hyssop, and I shall be clean; wash me, and I shall be whiter than snow' (51.7).

Within the context of God's covenant promise of grace, and covenant expectation of loyal love, it is absurd to interpret the washings with water as *merely* ceremonial or ritual. There is, of course, a tendency in all religious life towards mere externalism and it occurred all too frequently in Israelite history. But the story of the covenant demonstrates clearly that from the outset the covenant purpose acknowledged the distinction between, but maintained the closest relationship between, the outward and inward, the ceremonial and spiritual, the ritual and moral, the sign and the reality. It is there in the covenant with Abraham and Moses. It is then reinforced by prophets and psalmists — 'Who may stand in God's holy place? He who has clean hands and a pure heart' (Psalm 24.3,4).

The tendency to a mere externalism was frequently found in the Pharisee tradition, and Jesus ruthlessly attacks it. 'Woe to you, hypocrites! You clean the outside of the cup and dish, but inside they are full of greed and self-indulgence . . . first clean the inside . . . then the outside also will be clean' (Matthew 23.25f). 'Blessed are the pure in heart' (Matthew 5.8). Yet Jesus does not thereby indicate disapproval of outward rites or ceremonies. On the contrary, he not only identified himself with the baptizing ministry of John, but also provoked the Pharisees towards acknowledging that John's baptism was 'from heaven', and with the authority of God (Mark 11.30f).

The ceremonial washings of purification were used repeatedly and throughout life, and so, in that respect are quite distinct from a single washing which marks a distinctive, unique and once-for-all initiation into a new relationship and way of life. This concept is to be found emerging later.

Around the middle of the second century BC groups within Judaism developed strong traditions of very frequent washing with water which clearly combined concern for ceremonial and moral purity. The *Manual of Discipline* from the Dead Sea Scrolls demonstrates the pattern in the Qumran community, and other Essene groups had similar practice. In general these are frequently repeated, although there are clear signs of a development towards an initiatory washing which 'admits to the covenant of the community for ever'.[3]

Jewish baptism of proselytes

From the very beginning of the covenant with Abraham, foreigners could be brought within the covenant, and receive the sign of circumcision. Originally this provision appears to have been directed towards household slaves (Genesis 17.12f). The provision is reinforced in Exodus 12.48 which explains how foreigners can share in the Lord's Passover.

At some point these God-fearing Gentiles were required to submit also to a special washing or baptism. The date of this development is unclear, but it is widely accepted that although detailed evidence dates from the second century AD, there is clear evidence for proselyte baptism in the first century AD (and probably pre-70) as an already well-established custom.[4] Flemington argues the likelihood for this Jewish baptism being widely known before the ministry of John because, in the Gospels, the baptism of John is introduced without any explanation of its meaning.[5] Also, in view of the later bitterness between Jew and Christian, it is highly unlikely that the Jews would have borrowed baptism from the Christians or even from John. It is very likely, then, that Jewish proselyte baptism was of some influence on John's ministry.

This washing with water was increasingly seen (especially in the rabbinic school of Hillel) as *the* decisive mark of conversion to Judaism. After confessing faith in the God of Israel in the presence of witnesses the convert experienced the baptism-washing and so became 'a child of the covenant'. The Rabbis used the language of regeneration — the convert is 'like a child newly born'. It was an initiation into a new life to be lived according to the law of the living God.

It is not clear how and why this requirement became established and even dominant in conversion to Judaism. There was the strong tradition that Gentiles were 'unclean' (morally and ceremonially), and the law of God provided regulations of washing for purification, as seen in the last section. Further, women converts increased in number, and came into Judaism independently of their husbands. Thus the initiatory washing with water became increasingly appropriate. The rabbinic traditions of the second century AD indicate that it was taken for granted that children, including the very young, would share the baptism-washing and be received into the Jewish faith, into the covenant.

The baptism of John

The ministry of John was clearly of very great significance. The Gospel writers unite in describing his preaching and baptizing as 'the beginning of the good news' and a mark of the nearness of God's kingdom. Jesus supports John's ministry, and even requests his baptism. He regarded John as the promised Elijah of Malachi 4.5f who was to 'turn the hearts' of people before 'the great and terrible day of the Lord' (Mark 9.13; Matthew 11.14; Luke 1.17). In Jesus' estimation he was the last and greatest of the prophetic men of God, and yet as one only standing (as it were) on the doorstep of the kingdom, he was (in respect of those new covenant privileges) less than the least in the kingdom (Matthew 11.1–13). His baptizing activity not only gave him his extra name but provided the starting point for apostolic preaching (Acts 10.37; 13.24f; cf. 1.22).

In view of the significance of this baptizing ministry in the estimation of Jesus, the evangelists and the apostles, and in view of Jesus himself undergoing John's baptism, indicating its divine authority (Mark 11.30f) and, with his disciples, continuing some such ceremony (John 3.22, 26; 4.1), this baptism of John is a crucially important antecedent to Christian baptism. The chief references are Mark 1.1–8; Matthew 3.1–12; Luke 3.1–17; John 1.26f, 32f. Matthew's key verses are:

> John said: I baptize you with water for repentance. But after me will come one who is more powerful than I, whose sandals I am not fit to carry. He will baptize you with the Holy Spirit and with fire. His winnowing fork is in his hand, and he will clear his threshing floor, gathering the wheat into his barn and burning up the chaff with unquenchable fire. (3.11–12).

Some scholars consider that John's baptism was itself the commencement of Christian baptism.[6] This is unlikely for the following reasons: (a) John's baptism was not explicitly 'in the name of Jesus'; (b) it was not a baptism of the Spirit, and John sharply contrasts his baptizing and the subsequent baptizing of the Messiah on this very point; (c) how can there be Christian baptism until Jesus has undergone his baptism of the cross, and poured out his baptism of the Spirit at Pentecost?; (d) the disciples at Ephesus (Acts 19.1–7) had received John's baptism but did not know the Holy Spirit. After instruction by Paul they were baptized 'into the name of the Lord Jesus' and the Holy Spirit came on them. On the other hand we have no record of the original disciples being baptized with water after Jesus' death, resurrection and gift of the Spirit. Nor are we told of Apollos, who knew only the baptism of John, receiving another baptism into Christ. However, these points scarcely overthrow the weight of the earlier arguments and it is worth remembering that in the early church there was considerable variety of practice in matters of ministry and ceremony.

What, then, is the meaning of John's washing with

water, his baptism? There are three characteristics — purification, initiation and preparation.

1. *Purification.* John's baptism was about cleansing. It was a ceremony with water that was inseparably linked to preaching about God's kingdom-reign, and specifically the appeal to *repentance*. This word means a change of heart and mind, a turning around, a conversion. When the hearers experienced this conversion they confessed their sins, were baptized with water, and were assured of forgiveness. The baptism of John involved the outward use of water, an obvious and historic symbol of washing and purification, and the inward spiritual and moral appeal for, and response of, turning from sin to God's way. There is the closest possible connection between the symbol and the reality. God gave John the verbal message and God gave John the visual message (John 1.33).

It is certainly true that John emphatically contrasts his baptism with water and the Messianic baptism with Spirit, but careful questions must be asked about the point of the contrast. As has already been noted with regard to the relation between 'old' and 'new' covenant (p. 48), superficial contrasts are all too easily made that neglect the full evidence. For instance, it is frequently asserted[7] that John's baptism is merely outward as opposed to Jesus' inward baptism through and with the Spirit. But how can a baptism of repentance, conversion, confession and forgiveness be described as merely outward? Surely this is the work of the Spirit of God, as it has been noted he was working throughout the Old Testament phase of the story of God's covenant. The Spirit obviously does not appear for the first time at Pentecost nor even at the baptism (or even the conception) of Jesus.

The point of the contrast is to be found elsewhere, as will be seen. It is not to be found by making

John's baptism into an external ritual and ceremony with water alone. Such a view contradicts his entire message and purpose. His ministry is spiritual and moral through and through — in its initial call for repentance, in its warning of divine judgement, and in its careful and detailed teaching of the practical implications of repentance in daily life, (Luke 3.10–14). It is a baptism of purification and cleansing of heart and mind with the sign of water-washing.

2. *Initiation*. John's baptism seems to have been a single experience rather than a repeated and frequent one. With regard to this aspect it was unlike the oft-repeated Jewish washings of the Mosaic covenant-law, and more like the Jewish washing of Gentile proselytes. It has the character of initiation, a mark of entry into a new way of life.

The Jews, as we have seen, had probably established the custom that God-fearing Gentiles who wished to become children of the covenant, and members of God's people needed to mark this decisive step by a washing. John now makes the scandalous proposal that the people of Israel themselves are 'unclean' and need cleansing, that they are outside of the covenant through their faithlessness and need decisively to renew it, that to be racially Israelite is (in the final analysis) spiritually irrelevant (Luke 3.8) and they need to become truly the people of God. This requires a decisive change of attitude — hence the appropriateness of a ceremony of initiation which symbolizes what God offers and what they receive. The very ceremony devised for those outside the covenant is now offered to those who prided themselves on being the covenant people. The barrier between God and his people is once again explicitly seen to be a matter of sin rather than of race — spiritual and moral rather than national.

This had always been so, as the covenant story

throughout the Old Testament demonstrates. This is not a new theology, but the old covenant theology re-applied with the typically prophetic pungency that comes from a sharp contemporary application of God's ancient message.

3. *Preparation*. John was a great prophet — and a truly humble man. He knew, and made it very clear to his hearers, that he was preparing the way for one incomparably greater than he. He accepted that the Messiah's role would increase and his role decrease. John's characteristic ministry is a water-baptism involving repentance and forgiveness of sins, and he highlights the contrast between forerunner and Messiah at this very point of baptism. His water baptism was a preparation for the Messiah who will baptize with Holy Spirit and fire. What does that mean?

The arguments by various critical scholars against the authenticity of John's words about the Holy Spirit are unconvincing, and all four gospels give unanimous testimony at this point.[8]

It is easy to explain the Messianic baptism of the Spirit as a reference to the disciples' experience on the Day of Pentecost, but what about the 'fire'? Matthew and Luke both immediately go on to speak of the judgement ministry of Jesus — 'his winnowing fork is in his hand, and he will clear his threshing floor, gathering the wheat into his barn and burning up the chaff with unquenchable fire' (Matthew 3.12; Luke 3.17). This probably refers to the 'coming wrath' of Luke 3.7, a day of judgement, (cf. v.9). Because of this judgement context it is difficult to believe the fire refers to 'what seemed to be tongues of fire that separated and came to rest on each' of the disciples at the baptism with Spirit at Pentecost (Acts 2.3).

Does the baptism of Spirit and fire refer to two baptisms — one of Spirit to Jesus' followers and one of fiery judgement to the wicked? Or does it refer to one fiery Spirit baptism which involves both blessing and judgement at one and the same time?[9] Spirit and fire are linked together at Isaiah 4.4 as a judgement in the context of washing and cleansing (cf. Malachi 3.2f). Perhaps then it refers to one great act of purifying judgement by which God's people will be sanctified and obdurate rebels destroyed. This great baptism may incorporate the crucial salvation-judgement complex of events of Calvary to Pentecost. The baptism of blood and judgement fire of the cross is intimately linked to the baptism of Spirit at Pentecost, and both will reach their consummation at the Parousia, the return of Jesus Christ as Lord and Judge.

To summarize: John's baptism was essentially preparatory, and pointing towards the supreme salvation-events of the cross, Pentecost and ultimately the Parousia of the Messiah. In this sense he brings down the curtain on the Old Testament era of 'promise', and stands at the doorstep of the new covenant Messianic era of 'fulfilment'. Yet his baptizing-renewal ministry is in the great prophetic tradition of recalling the people to spiritual and moral conversion of heart. This is no merely outward and ceremonial matter — the sign of baptism with water is totally identified with the reality of which it eloquently speaks. John's verbal and visual message was a means of initiation into the renewed covenant community that precisely did *not* put any confidence in the outward and racial, but solely in the inward and spiritual conversion that would lead to a radically different life-style.

This is a baptism of real purification (by God's grace) and of real initiation (into God's covenant life), while still having the nature of the partial and the temporary because it is a preparation for the baptism of completion and permanence — the fulfilment in Christ.

5

Jesus and baptism

The most remarkable baptism by John was when Jesus himself came from Nazareth and was baptized in the river Jordan. We have already seen that John's baptism was, in one respect, preparatory and looking forward to a mightier One who would exercise a mightier baptism. One of the reasons that God called John to this ministry was so that the mightier One 'might be revealed to Israel' (John 1.31). This happened at his baptism.

The biblical references are Mark 1.9–11; Matthew 3.13–17; Luke 3.21–22. The fullest account is in Matthew's gospel:

> Then Jesus came from Galilee to the Jordan to be baptized by John. But John tried to deter him, saying, 'I need to be baptized by you, and do you come to me?' Jesus replied, 'Let it be so now; it is proper for us to do this to fulfil all righteousness'. Then John consented. As soon as Jesus was baptized, he went up out of the water. At that moment heaven was opened, and he saw the Spirit of God descending like a dove and lighting on him. And a voice from heaven said, 'This is my Son, whom I love; with him I am well pleased'.

The Markan account has only minor variations, e.g. the words from heaven are addressed *to* Jesus. This is so in Luke too. In his account Jesus is characteristically praying immediately after the baptism when he receives the vision. The Fourth Gospel does not describe the actual baptism of Jesus at all (nor the following temptations). The writer presupposes his readers know about Jesus' baptism, and John 1.29–34 is very relevant. In each gospel the account immediately follows the description of John's general ministry of preaching and baptizing.

Why was Jesus baptized? The first and clearest characteristic of John's baptism was that it was for repentance and involved confession and forgiveness of sins. It was a baptism of cleansing and conversion. Furthermore, it implied that the covenant with God required renewal through a decisive change of attitude marked by a ceremony of initiation into this new spiritual relationship.

It is not surprising that through the centuries Christians have been perplexed by this question. Matthew alone records (3.14) John's anxiety about the request, and presumably (even before the revelation in the baptism itself) he had a strong feeling that Jesus was (at the very least) a greater prophet for whom he was preparing the way. Jesus' reply to his attempt at dissuasion is 'It is proper for us to do this to fulfil all righteousness' i.e. to do all that God requires. Jesus later described John's preaching as showing people 'the way of righteousness' and enabling them to 'enter the kingdom of God' (Matthew 21.31f). This righteousness is God's right way, God's plan for people's lives. Jesus knew that God had a special plan for his life. A sign of this awareness emerged when, aged twelve, he went up to the Temple (Luke 2.41–52). Although it is fruitless to speculate about Jesus' psychology of growing self-consciousness, his understanding of his own person and vocation was presumably nurtured by the reading of, and meditation on, the Scriptures. It is certainly clear that his baptism marked the flowering and affirmation of his self-understanding and acceptance of his person and ministry. As he explained to the disciples 'My food is to do the will of him who sent me and to finish his work' (John 4.34).

Did Jesus' baptism include repentance for his own personal sin? The apostolic witness gives no indication that this is so, and many indications to the contrary. Jesus is described as one who is totally obedient to the Father, and for whom the fulfilment of Scripture is an utmost priority. He is inflexible in his opposition to the Evil One, and his greatest concern is the glory of God, the kingdom of God and the will of God. The biblical testimony to the reality of his humanity and yet the sinlessness of his character is summarized in Hebrews 4.15 'We do not have a high priest (Jesus) who is unable to sympathize with our weaknesses, but we have one who has been tempted in every way, just as we are — yet was without sin'.

There can be no doubt that one reason for Jesus coming to John at the Jordan was to identify himself with John's ministry, to acknowledge its divine authority, and to participate in the 'covenant-renewal' movement amongst the people in response to John's preaching.

However, there are more profound theological issues revealed in Jesus' baptism which relate to his person and vocation as known and accepted by himself and as revealed to those with 'ears to hear'. It is not only pedantic but contrary to the apostolic witness to draw any line between the baptism with water in the river and the subsequent anointing with the Spirit and the words from heaven.[1] The attempt to drive any wedge between the washing with the water and the Spirit-anointing and heavenly affirmation does not arise out of the text of the Synoptic Gospels. There is the closest possible relationship there — and it is precisely that juxtaposition of theological issues which needs to be explored, not by imposing a divorce but by enquiring into the intimacy of the relationship.

Four major theological issues clearly emerge — Jesus' identification with sinners, his commitment to a sacrificial death, the Spirit's anointing and the heavenly assurance of sonship.

Identification with sinners

It was John's baptism with water that Jesus requested, John's baptism that would point to the fulfilment of all that God required in Jesus' life — and John's baptism was for sinners. Jesus identified himself with sinful humanity in spite of his own perfect obedience. Paradoxically, this identification with sinners was a supreme example of that perfect obedience.

The messianic hope of the Old Testament developed towards an individual who would be strikingly different from, and yet closely identified with, the people who needed forgiveness and salvation. The servant of the Lord was 'numbered with the transgressors' (Isaiah 53.12, cf. Luke 22.37). In fulfilment of this messianic promise, Jesus took the very nature of a servant, and became a man in full reality — the Word became flesh (Philippians 2.7; John 1.14). Throughout his public ministry he went out of his way to be a friend to outcasts and to sinners, to mix with, touch, and bring God's mercy to, those who were unclean — not just ceremonially, but, in truth, morally too. Time and again he condemned the religious (self-) righteousness of Scribes and Pharisees and emphasized that he had come for the sick, the lost, the outsider, the poor and those who mourn. The One who in life befriended the Samaritan woman, Zaccheus and Mary of Magdala, in death accompanied two robbers in an execution for the worst kind of criminal.

Because he came to help human beings 'he had to be made like his brothers in every way' (Hebrews 2.17). As identified with, and representative of, humanity, he was called the 'last Adam' (1 Corinthians 15.45). As identified with, and representative of, God's covenant-breaking people of Israel, he too passed through the water and went into the desert for testing.

Here, in the baptism for sinners, Jesus unambiguously affirms his identification with rebellious and covenant-breaking humanity — an identification planned in eternity, prophesied in the Old Testament, unveiled in the incarnation, demonstrated in his public ministry and fulfilled in his execution.

Commitment to sacrificial death

The identification of Jesus with sinful humanity went far beyond incarnation, human frailty and a martyr's death — it embraced the consequences and penalty of that rebellion. Baptism is clearly a symbol to Jesus of death — not ordinary death but sacrificial death i.e. for others and for sin. By a decision and action of indescribable compassion and humiliation, Jesus, not only identified himself with sinners in their humanness but in their sinfulness. He was identified with the rebellion against Almighty God and took it into himself and upon himself. Paul explained that 'God made him who had no sin to be sin for us' (2 Corinthians 5.21). But is this a later theological development rather than part of the meaning of Jesus' baptism?

When James and John asked for special positions in heaven's glory, Jesus replied 'Can you drink the cup I drink or be baptized with the baptism I am baptized with?' (Mark 10.35ff). The 'cup' is a much used Old Testament symbol of the wrath of God in judgement against sin (see Psalms 75.8; Isaiah 51.17–23; Jeremiah 25.15–28; Habakkuk 2.16). In the Garden of Gethsemane, Jesus prayed 'Take this cup from me' (Mark 14.36) referring to his death at Calvary and experience of desolation as he knew the curse of the divine holiness. A little earlier at the Supper he had taken the cup and explained its significance in terms of blood poured out for many and blood for covenant renewal. The being overwhelmed in baptism is a parallel to the bitter dregs of the cup. James and John misunderstood the depths of Jesus' words and answered that they could participate. They were probably thinking of the glories of martyrdom, and had no understanding yet of Jesus giving his life as a ransom for many (Mark 10.45).

This interpretation is confirmed in the light of Luke 12.49–51 where Jesus again speaks of baptism metaphorically: 'I have come to bring fire on the earth, and how I wish it were already kindled. But I have a baptism to undergo, and how distressed I am until it is completed!' This baptism is a coming ordeal which is consuming his mind and governing all his thought and action. Only his death on the cross fits. Jesus is to pass through a baptism, an ordeal, a flood of unimaginable pain and suffering — not primarily the physical which was shared by many, but the spiritual alienation and desolation of a sacrificial victim. The prospect of this suffering was a perpetual Gethsemane. 'My heart is troubled, and what shall I say? "Father save me from his hour?" No, it was for this very reason I came to this hour' (John 12.27).

Baptism and fire have already been linked by John in his prophecy of Jesus' new kind of baptism (see p. 59). It was suggested there (and this passage supports the interpretation) that the baptism of Spirit and fire was the complex of salvation-judgement events from Calvary to Pentecost. But before the refining and judgement fire can be truly kindled and have its effects, Jesus must be plunged in the flood of pain and sorrow.

The final words from the heavenly voice following the baptism 'with him I am well pleased' are a clear reference to Isaiah 42.1, especially since the anointing with the Spirit is in both immediate contexts. This refers to the Servant of the Lord, the suffering servant, whose vocation was to be stricken by God, pierced for transgressions and bearing the punishment that brings peace — he carried the sins of many (Isaiah 53.4,5,12). Thus, the baptism of Jesus is understood by him and confirmed by the voice of God as a symbol of the overwhelming experience of death as a sacrifice for sin. The One more powerful than John who will baptize with Spirit and fire will first be led by that same Spirit into the baptism of fire — a baptism of the holy wrath of God, which involves both judgement and salvation.

Although the Fourth Gospel does not have a baptism narrative comparable to the Synoptic gospels, the writer in John 1.29–34 clearly presupposes knowledge of the event and refers to the theologically significant aspects. It is an obviously baptismal context with three references to baptism and clear references to the descent of the Spirit and the heavenly affirmation of sonship. It is surely of real significance that in this strongly baptismal context John's first words are 'Look, the Lamb of God, who takes away the sin of the world'. Why does John use the description 'lamb (amnos) of God'? Many think instinctively of the Passover with which Jesus was later identified (1 Corinthians 5.7). This just might be in John's mind if he saw Jesus as leading the second and greater exodus, but the Greek word in 1 Corinthians 5.7 is pascha and does not refer to a lamb — the Passover victim could, and may well have been more frequently, a kid. Other suggestions are the lamb of the daily Temple sacrifice or the God-provided lamb of Genesis 22.8. This story was highly significant in Judaic thought, but the lamb was not obviously 'taking sin' although it was sacrificial. In view of the voice from heaven introducing the suffering Servant idea from Isaiah, it seems most likely that John has in mind the imagery of the lamb used in the Servant songs, notably Isaiah 53 — 'he was led like a lamb to the slaughter', verse 7. The themes of vicarious suffering and 'taking away the sins' of others is very strong throughout (verses 4–6, 8, 10–12). John recognizes that Jesus is the mightier One, that he is to fulfil the role of the Servant of the Lord, that this is to involve sacrificial suffering in order to effect a baptism of infinitely more significance than his washing in Jordan, and yet of which that very washing was a prophetic sign.

Thus, through the symbolism of baptism itself in Jesus' own consciousness, and through the confirming suffering Servant words from heaven and the similar understanding of John, it becomes apparent that in his baptism Jesus was committing himself to sacrificial death for the sin of the world. This was a commitment planned in eternity, prophesied in the Old Testament, unveiled in the Incarnation ('You are to give him the name Jesus, because he will save his people from their sins', Matthew, 1.21), frequently predicted during, and the supreme purpose of, his earthly ministry, and fulfilled at the cross of Calvary — 'My God, why have you abandoned me?' (Matthew 27.46 quoting Psalms 22.1).

Spirit anointing

The coming down of the Spirit on Jesus was of the greatest significance to the four gospel writers or editors. Jesus was known throughout the early Church as the Anointed One (Messiah in Hebrew, Christos in Greek). The dramatic significance is heightened by the reference in all three Synoptics to the heavens being opened ('torn apart' in Mark) — and in John the Spirit came down from heaven. This is a famous Old Testament mark of God's intervention (see Isaiah 64.1). Throughout the Old Testament period the Holy Spirit was at work, coming upon particular people for special responsibility or service. In chapter 2 we saw that anointing was associated with the outpouring of the Spirit (pp. 25, 27), particularly on kings, prophets and priests. As the messianic hope of a covenant-restoring ruler in the line of David developed so did the prophetic understanding that he would be uniquely the recipient of the Spirit of the Lord with his graces and gifts (Isaiah 11.1–2 and 61.1–3 read by Jesus in the Nazareth synagogue after which he said 'Today this Scripture is fulfilled in your hearing', Luke 4.16–21).

The Holy Spirit descended on him 'like a dove'. This Jewish symbol could derive from 'the Spirit of God hovering over the waters' at the very beginning of creation, Genesis 1.2. It could also derive from Noah's use of a dove to establish the ending of the flood and the beginning of the new era after the catastrophic judgement, Genesis 8.8–12. The flood story certainly was used to symbolize and illustrate baptism (1 Peter 3.20f). In both cases the symbolism expresses initiation — creation, and a new covenant era. At Jesus' baptism the Holy Spirit, symbolized in the dove, speaks of a new creation by the Spirit, and a new covenant era inaugurated through the Spirit.

Anointing with the Holy Spirit, being 'Christ-ed', has the double significance of (a) consecration, being set apart for a holy purpose, and (b) being empowered and equipped or gifted for the divine task. So, here in the baptism, in an obvious and dramatic way Jesus consecrates himself to the will of God, and God consecrates him for his public ministry and supreme vocation. The Father had already set him apart as his very own and sent him into the world, and Jesus nearing the cross was to say 'For them (the disciples) I sanctify myself, that they too may be truly sanctified' (John 10.36; 17.19).

This was how the apostles understood the coming of the Holy Spirit at the baptism. We have seen something of the significance of 'sealing' with respect to both baptism and the Holy Spirit (pp. 24, 27). So when Jesus says of the Son of Man 'on him God the Father has placed his seal of approval' (John 6.27) the sentiment is true generally but must be focused on the baptism initiation-cum-ordination to public ministry. The early Christians spoke of Jesus as God's holy servant who was anointed with the Holy Spirit and power (Acts 4.27; 10.38).

A renewed and widespread work of the Holy Spirit had long been part of the prophetic hope and proclamation of a new covenant and new era (Joel 2.28; Ezekiel 37.1–14 noting that the Hebrew word *ruach* means Spirit and breath; 36.26f; Isaiah 63.7ff especially 10–14). The anointing of Jesus with the Spirit is the inauguration of the baptism of the Spirit that will mark the new covenant, the ministry of the Anointed One and the character of the kingdom of God, the era that is to come.

In the baptism of Jesus is dramatically displayed in history an anointing with the Spirit by the Father upon the Son which was planned in eternity in the mysterious loving counsels of the Triune God. It was foretold in the Old Testament, unveiled in the Incarnation (Matthew 1.20; Luke 1.35), continually experienced throughout his ministry, and finally demonstrated with power in the resurrection (Acts 2.36).

Sonship assured

In the three synoptic gospels the voice is 'from heaven' i.e. this is God speaking with solemnity and authority at a significant moment in salvation-history and revelation. At this point of Jesus' acceptance of his vocation and God's anointing of him to that vocation, the divine message comes in the terms of the coronation formula of the king of Israel — 'You are my Son' (Psalm 2.7). The Son is the Lord's Anointed One, the King of God's people. Although John omits the actual baptism, he specifically mentions within the baptismal section that the One on whom the Spirit descended is the Son of God (John 1.34). The relationship of Jesus to God the Father is unique, though analogous to that of the anointed king of Israel. It did not date from the baptism for it had previously been announced to his mother Mary (Luke 1.35). The uniqueness of the relationship was understood by Jesus and explained in his teaching (Matthew 11.25f; Luke 10.21f; John 10.38; 14.9 and many other places in the gospels).

The writer to the Hebrews develops the theme of Jesus' unique Sonship in the light of the covenant story with the kings of Israel whose vocation was to keep the people in covenant with God as his precious possession.

But the divine voice goes on to add the ordination formula of the Servant of the Lord (Isaiah 42.1). This means that the king is to be a suffering Son on behalf of the people as we have seen earlier. Jesus clearly hinted at this kind of Sonship in the parable of the tenants (Matthew 21.33ff).

The unique Sonship of Jesus is affirmed in the baptism. However, through the Logos, the Word, it had an eternal reality, was unveiled in the Incarnation, was a constant feature of Jesus' consciousness in his ministry, and finally vindicated in his exaltation to the right hand of glory.

These four major theological motifs clearly emerge from Jesus' baptism. Although the fourth gospel contains no account of the baptism itself, it develops the latter three issues in a clearly baptismal context which obviously refers to the baptism of Jesus in Jordan.

Jesus chose baptism with water as the vehicle to express his identification with sinners and commitment to a sacrificial death for them. God chose the baptism as the occasion in which to anoint him with the Holy Spirit and assure him of his unique divine Sonship. There is, once again, the closest possible relationship between the outward and visible symbols and the inward and spiritual realities.

We have noted previously that Jesus and his disciples practised a baptizing ministry themselves although we know very little about it (John 3.22ff; 4.1ff). We have also seen how Jesus thought of his own impending death as a baptism (Mark 10.38; Luke 12.50). Finally back in chapter 2 (p. 14) we looked briefly at the risen Lord's great commission (Matthew 28.19–20) where baptism is set firmly in the context of making disciples through evangelism and nurturing them in the faith — which brings us to the early church.

6
Christian baptism

Christian baptism is intimately related to and dependent upon the baptism of blood suffered by Jesus Christ on the cross, and the baptism of Spirit poured out by Jesus on the Day of Pentecost. The evidence for the early Christian *practice* of baptism is found primarily in the Acts of the Apostles, and for the early Christian *theology* of baptism primarily in the epistles of the New Testament.

In chapter 2 we listed the nine instances of Christian baptism in the Acts and noted the five distinctive features associated with it:

- it is 'in the name of Jesus Christ' implying allegiance to, and union with him;
- it is closely linked to preaching of the gospel and making disciples;
- it involves repentance and faith and leads to forgiveness of sins;
- it usually (though not always) includes the gift of the Holy Spirit;
- it usually implies incorporation into the church.

Also in chapter 2 we considered the nine explicit passages and eight probable references in the epistles which speak of Christian baptism.

This material can now be interpreted in the light of the covenant context, the baptism ministry of John and the baptism experience of Jesus. The theology of Christian baptism which emerges from this material will be developed in terms of:

- the blessings of baptism
- the context of baptism
- the effect of baptism

and consideration will also be given to the relation of 'word' and 'action'.

There is *one* baptism (Ephesians 4.5) into the one and only Lord Jesus Christ. Thus there can be only one true theology of baptism. There cannot be (and certainly is not in the New Testament) a theology of adult baptism and a different theology of household (infant) baptism. If there is any justification for family baptism which includes infants, it must (if it is to be biblical) be based on the one theology of baptism. It has been a grave and fatal weakness of so many studies on infant baptism that they have developed a separate and distinctive theological understanding. The theology here will be developed in terms of the biblical evidence alone with no appeal to post-apostolic tradition, church history or confessional statements. In the next chapter we will ask the specific question as to whether that biblical theology sustains Christian household baptism or not, but it is a vital methodological issue that the question is posed in those terms and those terms alone. This is the only path for a truly biblical theology, and the only path for secure progress in ecumenical theology.

Furthermore the one baptism reminds us that Christian baptism does not belong to any Christian tradition — Catholic, Orthodox, Anglican, Baptist or any other. It belongs to the one Lord, the one Spirit, and the one God and Father of all, who is over all and through all and in all.

Baptism is, by its very nature, once-for-all. It marks the beginning of Christian life, it is Christian initiation. Christians may, indeed should, make progress in understanding the meaning of baptism and Christian discipleship, they may at a later stage receive a new and bright illumination or take a major step forward in discipleship, they may return to Christ after failure or even apostasy, but never again can they *begin* Christian life. Thus 're-baptism' or 'second baptism' is, in the strict sense of the term, non-sense — it is a self-contradiction. It is impossible. The issue of the validity of a baptism of an unbeliever will be considered later in this chapter (p. 89), and the issue of 'believers' baptism' following an infant baptism in chapter 10.

Before we embark on the three main aspects of the theology of Christian baptism, it is important to remember the biblical claim that human life is lived in one or other of two realms which are in dramatic and vivid contrast. We may be members of the old creation or the new creation, either in Adam or in Christ, in darkness or in light, living according to the sinful nature or by the Spirit, in death or in life, belonging to the world or belonging to God. These contrasts will be found in 2 Corinthians 5.17; 1 Corinthians 15.22; Ephesians 5.8 (cf. Colossians 1.13); Romans 8.5f; 1 John 3.14 (cf. John 10.10); John 17.6–19. However, although the conversion from one realm to the other is critical, and theologically a contrast that cannot be exaggerated, nevertheless from the human point of view that conversion may be a long, gradual and almost imperceptible process rather than a single, dramatic event. The New Testament writers nowhere require a sudden conversion experience, but do require convertedness — 'Unless you change (literally 'turn') and become like little children, you will never enter the kingdom of heaven' (Matthew 18.3).

Conversion means to turn around, to face the right direction, to be following Christ. The significant issue is not *when* or *how* but *whether* a person is going in the right direction i.e. is converted (Acts 3.19; 26.18). The metaphor of 'being born again' (John 3) is more to do with the decisively new character of life with God than with the suddenness of its arrival in human experience.

Baptism is, by its very nature, a single definite

event, but the human experience of conversion is not always (or even often) like that. Hence the relationship in time between baptism (the outward sign) and conversion (the spiritual reality) is not always a simple, obvious and straightforward one — as we shall see.

The blessings of baptism are:

1. Forgiveness and cleansing — 'Repent and be baptized . . . so that your sins may be forgiven' (Acts 2.38). 'Be baptized and wash your sins away' (Acts 22.16; see also 1 Corinthians 6.11; Ephesians 5.26; Hebrews 10.22; Titus 3.5).

2. Belonging to and being identified with Jesus Christ — Baptism is frequently described as 'in (into, Greek eis) the name of Jesus Christ' (Acts 2.38; Romans 6.3).

3. Sharing in the death and resurrection of Jesus Christ — 'baptized into his death . . . buried with him through baptism into death . . . united with him in his death . . . united with him in his resurrection' (Romans 6.3–5; Colossians 2.12).

4. The gift of the Holy Spirit — We have seen that John contrasted his water-baptism with the coming Messiah's Spirit-baptism (Matthew 3.11), so that one might even expect that after the Messianic baptism with the Spirit at Pentecost water-baptism might be discontinued. But the command of the risen Lord was otherwise, and Peter said 'Repent and be baptized . . . and you will receive the gift of the Holy Spirit' implying that water-baptism symbolizes Spirit-baptism. The pouring of the water dramatizes the outpouring of the Spirit (Acts 2.38; 1.5; Titus 3.5). This gift is a seal, a deposit, a guarantee assuring the inheritance of God's people until the final day of

redemption (2 Corinthians 1.21f; Ephesians 4.30; 1.13f). This baptism is the mark both of present experience and a future hope, a realized indwelling and an anticipated consummation.

5. New birth to adoption and sonship — 'He saved us by the washing of rebirth'. 'Sons of God through faith . . . for all of you who were baptized into Christ have been clothed with Christ' (Titus 3.5f; Galatians 3.26f and possibly John 3.5).

6. Membership of the body of Christ — 'We were all baptized by one Spirit into one body' (1 Corinthians 12.13). This body is God's covenant community, his church. Baptism marks initiation into the church, the Christian fellowship.

Later in this chapter we shall see that all these blessings, symbolized in and associated with baptism, are also vitally related to faith in Jesus Christ. We shall enquire as to the effect of baptism in relation to these blessings and to faith. For the moment, we note that the entire gospel, the whole covenant grace, promises and blessings of Almighty God are intimately expressed in baptism.

Comparison with the significance of John's baptism and the baptism of Jesus shows both continuity and development.

Before we expound the major issue of the effectiveness or efficacy of baptism in relation to the blessings it represents, there are two other matters carefully to be considered: the context of baptism, and the biblical pattern of word and action.

The context of baptism

Far too much theology of baptism is developed from small references of texts considered out of relation to their contexts. These contexts are not only *literary*, i.e. the setting within the 'Acts' or the epistles, but also *historical* i.e. within the early church experience, and *theological*, i.e. within an overall pattern of Christian faith and teaching. There are three outstanding features in the contexts of early Christian baptism:

1. *The Gospel*, its proclamation and reception — an evangelical context. It may seem too obvious to say that all nine references to baptism in the 'Acts' are explicitly in the context of preaching the good news of Jesus. It is always missionary baptism. It is indissolubly linked to making disciples.

However, the gospel context is not simply the preaching of Christ's gospel but also the reception of Christ's gospel by faith. It is of the greatest importance to recognize that each of the blessings signified in baptism (p. 76f) are similarly attributed to the word and its acceptance by *faith*:

(a) forgiveness and cleansing — 'He purified their hearts by faith' (Acts 15.9; see also 13.38f; Romans 3.21ff),
(b) identification with Christ — 'that Christ may dwell in your hearts through faith' (Ephesians 3.17),
(c) sharing the death and resurrection of Jesus — 'raised with him through your faith' (Colossians 2.12; Galatians 2.20),
(d) the gift of the Spirit — 'so that by faith we might receive the promise of the Spirit' (Galatians 3.14; 3.2; Ephesians 1.13),
(e) new birth and sonship — 'you are all sons of God through faith in Christ Jesus' (Galatians 3.26; John 1.12; James 1.18; 1 Peter 1.23f),
(f) membership of the church — 'we proclaim . . . so that you may have fellowship with us'. The church is 'the family of believers' (household of faith) (1 John 1.3; Galatians 6.10).

Thus it is clear that in the New Testament the word of the gospel and the sign of baptism are seen as a unity, and the same effects are attributed to both without contradiction or difference of meaning. The Presbyterian James Denney rightly said 'Baptism and faith are but the outside and the inside of the same thing',[1] and the Roman Catholic Schnackenburg wrote 'Baptism without faith in Christ is unimaginable for the thinking of the primitive church'.[2] It is not that faith makes human beings worthy of such blessings, or that baptism has an intrinsic power to produce them; it is God who enables faith and gives baptism — and all the blessings are his alone. The blessings are only secondarily baptism-blessings or faith-blessings; primarily they are God's blessings. Beasley-Murray neatly says 'Baptism is the divinely appointed rendezvous of grace for faith'.[3] The New Testament theology of baptism and faith presupposes the missionary context and the administration of baptism to converts.

In the light of this emphasis on evangelism and faith, it is inevitable that baptism of converts will involve a confession of faith. However, it is intriguing that the New Testament writers nowhere indicate the significance of the baptism-event in terms of the convert's witness to others. Rather it is *God's* witness or seal to the convert. The baptized *life* is seen as a witness to others rather than the baptism-event.

2. *The Covenant*, God's promise — a theological context. Detailed consideration has already been given to this matter in chapter 2 when we were looking for the right place to start the theological enquiry. It was discovered that an outstanding feature of the baptism passages is their emphatic and varied use of Old Testament covenant situations to illustrate and clarify their doctrinal exposition and ethical application. It was found that this is no incidental or occasional

context, but regular and foundational to their thinking. This led (chapter 3) to a careful survey of the covenant theme through the biblical revelation. In the light of the weight and clarity of the evidence for this theological context, it is remarkable that so many theologians and writers totally ignore it.[4] This can only be explained either by a fear that such acknowledgement might offer some support for comparison with circumcision and perhaps infant baptism, or by such an emphasis on charismatic baptism of the Spirit that water-baptism pales into virtual insignificance.

Baptism is seen as a covenant sign, an initiation into God's covenant community. The whole biblical theology of God's covenant plan of salvation is the apostolic writers' context.

3. *Holiness*, and unity — an ethical context.
This emphasis in the contexts of the baptism passages also emerged clearly from the study in chapter 2. In every single passage, whether explicit or probable, the writers used baptism as a basis for, or illustration of, an appeal for holiness of life or the unity of God's people. Baptism is not simply a sign of God's saving action in the *past* (in Jesus' death, resurrection and gift of the Spirit) or God's saving action in the *present* (in the application of that eternal covenant plan to an individual's experience through regeneration and conversion), but also God's saving action in the *future* (in the Spirit's outworking of fruit of character and gifts of service, and pledge of final redemption). The Christian is summoned to live a baptismal life. Because he is baptized, say the apostolic writers, the Christian must live a pure life, realize Christ living within, put to death the old life and live out a resurrection life, live according to the Holy Spirit, as a child of God, a member of Christ's body. Having been initiated, the convert is called to live accordingly. Become what you are — baptized, believer, set apart for God, recipient of the covenant promise.

Word and action

In the daily life of all cultures and countries throughout recorded history, a significant action is frequently attached to a word or words in order to reinforce the meaning. A handshake is added to a word of welcome and a kiss to a word of love or affection. Standing and drinking a toast is added to words of loyalty or of congratulation. The giving and receiving of a ring are added to the words of marriage vows. This last example indicates the special significance of such an action where a solemn and binding agreement is involved. In biblical times the affixing of a seal often accompanied the words of an agreement. In the account of Boaz becoming the kinsman-redeemer to Naomi and Ruth, the story-teller explains that 'for the redemption and transfer of property to become final, one party took off his sandal and gave it to the other. This was the method of legalizing transactions in Israel' (Ruth 4.7).

The prophets of Israel made use of actions to accompany and dramatize their verbal message. Elisha used bow and arrows when speaking God's word to Jehoash, king of Israel (2 Kings 13.14ff). Jeremiah smashed a clay jar with his words of judgement to Judah and Jerusalem (Jeremiah 19). The prophet Agabus tied up his hands and feet with Paul's belt to accompany his prediction about the Jews arresting Paul (Acts 21.10ff). An extension of this principle of adding action to word is the taking of an oath or swearing a promise upon one's life ('cross my heart', or 'upon my life', or in biblical times 'God do so to me and more also . . .' i.e. deal very severely, Ruth 1.17; 1 Kings 19.2; 20.10).

God's word is always declared by the biblical writers to be totally dependable, and yet, in his condescending mercy, God repeatedly adds a confirming and dramatic action or sign to his words. He added the rainbow to the words to Noah about security from another flood devastation. He added circumcision to the words of covenant promise to Abraham and his household. In addition, God takes an oath by his own name, his nature, his very reality — 'I swear by myself, declares the Lord' (Genesis 22.16; Hebrews 6.13). He stakes his life upon the covenant promise when he passes between the pieces of the sacrifice (Genesis 15.17, see p. 36). So, in the era of the new covenant Jesus breaks the bread with the words 'This is my body', and offers the cup with the words 'This is my blood of the new covenant'. So also, baptism with water is added to the words of God's cleansing forgiveness and offer of new life through the Spirit.

The action expresses the word and embodies it. It shows dramatically what God has done in Christ and desires to do in human lives. Through much of Christian history the word 'sacrament' has been used to describe this combination of divine action and word. The Latin word sacramentum was used of the sacred oath of a soldier. The word is regarded with suspicion by some Christians because of anxiety about sacramental*ism* i.e. when it seems that the significance of the action alone is magnified to such an extent that the significance of the accompanying word and the believing response of the recipient is gravely undervalued. However, as we shall see in the next section, such an imbalance is a false, not a true, understanding of a sacrament.

An outward and visible action accompanying a word concerning an inward and spiritual reality can be described as a sacrament, God's solemn and confirmed promise. It is a physical sign of a spiritual grace. It is a gift of God accompanying a word from God.

Grace is not a thing to be conveyed or a power to be transferred (as it were by a pipe or an electric cable). Grace is essentially a personal relationship established by God. It describes his attitude and action of compassion and mercy. Baptism is a sacrament of grace — a means by which God's grace brings a personal relationship — 'I will be your God, and you will be my child'. An action accompanies the word of covenant promise — a covenant sign. There is a dramatic as well as verbal expression of God's grace.

So then we are ready to face the next issue:

The effect of baptism

The blessings signified by, and associated with, baptism cannot be exaggerated. They comprise the whole gospel of Jesus Christ and the covenant promises of God. What, then, is the effect of water-baptism in the biblical context of the gospel proclamation and reception by faith, and of the covenant plan of God, and of the incessant appeal for holiness of life? There have been four main answers to this question through the centuries:

it is unnecessary — it has no effect, and Christians need not bother with the physical sign if they experience the spiritual grace;

it is desirable as an expression of obedience to Jesus but not essential. It is not considered in terms of effect, and the sign merely symbolizes the spiritual reality;

it is essential — a sign which actually conveys the blessings and grace of God. This description of its effectiveness often makes the whole process seem to be automatic;

it is God's gift and normal Christian practice — a sign and seal of God's grace effecting what it signifies in the context of faith.

This issue underlies many bitter divisions and controversies — between Catholic and Protestant, and between those who only baptize confessing believers and those who baptize households, and amongst the latter between those who look for a credible faith-response and others who appear to be virtually indiscriminate. The debates and writings through the centuries have been sadly disfigured by caricature and misrepresentation of other positions. Far too often theologians begin with a confessional position or ecclesiastical practice and then select or bend the biblical evidence to suit the predetermined goal. This has had disastrous effects in the disciplines of biblical and systematic theology, in ecumenical relationships and in terms of pastoral practice. We shall examine the four answers listed, but in the reverse order —

1. *Baptism effects what it signifies, in the context of faith*. Labels can often be misleading, and mean different things to different people. Nevertheless broad classifications are necessary in historical and theological study. This view is often broadly described as 'Reformed' or 'Covenant'. It is the confessional position in both the Anglican 39 Articles of Religion and the Presbyterian Westminster Confession of Faith. However, both those theological confessions explicitly require that the Holy Scriptures be the final authority for faith and practice, and so the question must be pressed with complete integrity as to whether the biblical witness points to this theological answer.

Three major truths relevant to the issue have emerged from the enquiry into the baptism texts and contexts. Firstly, the New Testament writers use the *language of efficacy* repeatedly and without embarrassment. Baptism effects what it signifies. The outward sign is described in terms of the spiritual reality it signifies. 'We were buried with him through baptism', 'we were all baptized by one Spirit into one body'. 'baptism now saves you' (Romans 6.4; 1 Corinthians 12.13; 1 Peter 3.21). 'Be baptized and wash your sins away', 'all who were baptized into Christ have been clothed with Christ' (Acts 22.16; Galatians 3.27). This language of efficacy is not occasional or idiosyncratic, it is normal and characteristic of the biblical thought-world and varying types of literature. We have seen how strong is the tradition of adding a confirming sign or action to a solemn word of promise.

Secondly, the apostolic writers unanimously and explicitly speak of the context of the *gospel met by faith*. We have seen how the very blessings signified in baptism are also in the same apostolic writings indissolubly linked to the word of God received by faith. Thus, the blessings are not attached to water-baptism just as a mere ceremony — there must normally be the accompanying (in fact, preceding) words of interpretation, the gospel proclamation, and the accompanying context of a faith-response. The New Testament writers look for some evidence of the work of the Spirit through the gospel. 'You must be born again. The wind blows wherever it pleases. You *hear its sound*, but you cannot tell where it comes from or where it is going. So it is with everyone born of the Spirit' (John 3.7f). There is much we do not know about the Spirit's work, but we do 'hear its sound' i.e. experience its effect in people's lives. The people of Samaria 'believed Philip as he preached the good news of the kingdom of God and the name of Jesus Christ, they were baptized . . . Simon himself believed and was baptized'. Nevertheless, later on, Simon tried to purchase the ability to lay hands on people to receive the Spirit, and Peter sternly rebuked him 'You have no part or share in this ministry, because your heart is not right before God. Repent of this wickedness and pray to the Lord . . .' (Acts 8.9–24). Here we see that even baptism with a profession of faith does not effect a truly Christian life — there must be a continuing baptized life of repentance and trusting commitment.

The vital importance of this continuing faith-response to the covenant signs of God is spelled out vividly by Paul in 1 Corinthians 10. All the Israelites experienced the sign of the baptism 'into Moses in the cloud and in the sea. They all ate the same spiritual food and drank the same spiritual drink . . . Nevertheless, God was not pleased with most of them'. Paul is clearly warning that participation in the outward covenant signs or sacramental actions is not effectual unconditionally; they must be received with faith and obedience. As Richard Hooker neatly said, 'All receive not the grace of God which receive the sacraments of his grace'.[5] Gospel, faith and baptism must be kept closely bound together both in theological thought and in pastoral practice if we are to be true to the New Testament. Baptism is efficacious, i.e. it effects what it signifies, in the context of faith. The evidence will be seen in the fruit of the Spirit and his gifts.

Paul labours the point that it is neither the performance of ceremonies nor the observance of law that brings spiritual life and a right relationship with God. This comes only through God's grace received by faith (Romans 3.27–30; Galatians 2.15ff; Ephesians 2.8f; Philippians 3.4–9). However, we must guard against any impression that faith is the cause or basis of salvation. God's grace and God's covenant sign of his grace do not derive their power and effect from the faith of the recipient, they derive their power from God himself. Faith does *take* the grace that God offers, but faith does not *make* that grace.

Thirdly, the apostolic writers unitedly and naturally speak of baptism in the context of the *covenant plan of God*. The clear implication is that baptism is a covenant sign. Thus, it is essentially a gift from God witnessing to what he has done and intends to do, rather than a human action witnessing to the faith-response. It may actually imply such a witness to faith, but this is not part of the New Testament theology of baptism and is not its primary significance. Having said that, the covenant promises of God and covenant-signs of God must be received by faith. It has always been so, and there is no other way to benefit from or enjoy them.

There has been a historic polarization between a Protestant type of pietism which has placed almost its entire emphasis on the inward reality of regeneration/conversion through the work of the Spirit and seen the outward sign of baptism as having very minor importance, and the Catholic type of sacramentalism which appears to place almost its entire emphasis on the outward sign and to place very little on the word of the gospel, conversion and the response of faith.

In contrast to this dichotomy, the biblical theology gives strong emphasis to both the efficacy of baptism and the necessity of faith in the context of God's covenant. It is very significant that the report *Baptism, Eucharist and Ministry* claims 'The necessity of faith for the reception of the salvation embodied and set forth in baptism is acknowledged by all churches. Personal commitment is necessary for responsible membership in the body of Christ.[6]

Baptism is a pledge from God which confirms his word of promise. It is backed up by his own total faithfulness, the nature of his character. This promise and confirming sign need (in normal circumstances) to be received by faith. However, as we have seen, baptism is more than just a symbol. This covenant sign —[7]

(a) confirms the promises — adding solemn action and sign to the word of promise concerning forgiveness and the gift of the Spirit;

(b) confers a status — as an adopted child of God. The new *nature* of the child of God may well develop gradually, but the new *status* is signified and sealed in baptism. Naturalization in a new country brings a new citizenship status, but adopting the life-style of that new nation may take a longer time;

(c) conveys an inheritance — the kingdom of God. This is conveyed by baptism in a way analogous to the legal deed of conveyance used for transfer of land or property.

Note that the promise must be received, the status adopted, the inheritance claimed — by faith.

Another way of similarly describing the relation of baptism to God's covenant plan and promise of salvation is to say that baptism [8] —

(a) pictures it — as washing, as anointing, as burial and resurrection;
(b) promises it — the sign which dramatizes and confirms the word;
(c) presents it — in the context of gospel and faith, baptism embodies and effects the salvation it pictures and promises.

The faith which takes this promise and sign of God's salvation involves repentance, trust and obedience. It is not just a single act (a turning, a change, a conversion) but a continuing attitude (being turned to Christ, remaining changed and converted). This is the continuing character of the baptized life, the life that is baptized into Jesus Christ. As it was suggested earlier, the relation in time between the reception of the sign and the reception of the blessings signified is not always straightforward. Quite apart from the question of household-(infant) baptism which will be considered in the next chapter, in the baptism of an adult the ideal may well be conversion followed immediately by baptism. This seems the normal pattern in the early church. However, baptism may be delayed for many reasons until years after conversion because of antagonism of husband or family, or because of inadequate instruction. On the other hand, someone may be baptized before (even long before) conversion. This may be through family, peer or other pressures, or again because of inadequate instruction. Now, although when this happens in the case of an adult baptism it may be regarded as irregular and unfortunate, none of the major churches (including those with baptist theology who emphasize that personal confession of faith should precede baptism) will offer 'another' baptism. The original baptism is regarded as valid initiation which (by definition) can only, and must be, once-for-all. It may be improper and irregular but is regarded as 'valid'.

Although the concept of a valid or real baptism is not dealt with explicitly in the New Testament, from the earliest centuries Christian churches of all types have had to answer the question, 'When is a baptism a real baptism?' Although the *spiritual* reality or efficacy of the baptism depends on God's promise of grace met by faith, the reality of the *outward* sign cannot be made to depend on an inward and spiritual response. Ultimately, only God can judge the reality and sincerity of repentance, faith and obedience. Christians with tender consciences could repeatedly be anxious about their previous spiritual condition and apply for 'another' baptism. Christians who receive some fresh (even dramatic) experience of the reality and blessing of God are often unsure whether it is an initial conversion or a subsequent and further step in their pilgrimage.

What, then, makes a valid or real baptism in terms of the outward sign? Most churches agree that two elements are required. Baptism must be —

(a) an administration of water;

(b) in the name of God, the Father, Son and Holy Spirit or in the name of Jesus Christ, or with words that indicate it is *Christian* baptism.

Some (though not all) baptist churches add a third requirement;

(c) following a personal confession of faith in Jesus as Saviour and Lord.

However, as we noted above, even churches which baptize only adults and young people following a profession of faith find the necessity of distinguishing (spiritual) efficacy from (outward) validity. If validity of sign is made to depend on a spiritual state that only God can truly know, there will be perpetual potential for feelings of insecurity about its reality. We may sum up by saying that the outward sign of baptism as defined above is complete in terms of (outward) validity but conditional in terms of (spiritual) efficacy, i.e. it will require (in normal circumstances) the response of faith.

An example of the distinction between outward sign or ceremony and existing reality is to be found in the relationship between a monarch inheriting the throne and being formally crowned. Queen Elizabeth II inherited the throne on the death of her father but it was some months later that the existing reality of her monarchy was declared, confirmed and celebrated in the service of coronation. In one sense she really became queen on her accession, in another sense she was 'made queen' in the coronation ceremony. In this example, the reality precedes the ceremony or sign. However, in another case, the new monarch may be a child. In this situation, although on the one hand inheriting the throne and experiencing the ceremony of coronation, on the other hand the full enjoyment of rights, privileges and powers will follow later at an appropriate age of majority. This is *not* cited as an example to justify infant baptism. At this stage it is simply an example of how the outward sign or ceremony could precede the full enjoyment of the reality of the thing signified. This can and does happen in 'believer-baptism only' situations.

C. S. Lewis wrote, 'Don't bother at all about that question of a person being "made a Christian by baptism". It is only the usual trouble about a word being used in more than one sense. Thus we might say a man "became a soldier" the moment he joined the army. But his instructors might say six months later, "I think we have made a soldier of him".'[9]

We conclude then that the biblical theology of baptism is this:
Baptism is a covenant sign that God gives to confirm and seal his promise of salvation. It effects what it signifies, in the context of faith.

> Baptism requires conversion i.e. repentance and faith.
> Baptism shapes conversion i.e. in terms of washing, death and new life, and anointing with the Spirit.
> Baptism tests conversion i.e. ensuring it is 'into Christ'.[10]

The language of efficacy which the New Testament writers use with respect to baptism is sacramental language, covenant language. It is not unconditional for it presupposes the context of faith — sacramental language must always be faith language.

However, there are other views which need to be considered (see p. 83).

2. *Baptism always conveys the blessings of salvation*, in a way that appears almost automatic. This view has been held in order to safeguard the sovereignty of God's work of salvation, the divine initiative in both covenant promise and covenant sign and the power

of Christ's sacrifice. It takes very seriously the vigorous New Testament sacramental language of efficacy.

This view is broadly termed the 'Catholic' or *ex opere operato* view (a Latin phrase meaning 'by the deed performed' i.e. 'by the performance of the ceremony'). There was an exception to this automatic conveyance of the divine grace in baptism if an adult recipient placed a barrier (obex) or obstacle to it through mortal sin (e.g. impenitence or hypocrisy). However, the *ex opere operato* view gained supremacy during the later Middle Ages, and was endorsed by the Council of Trent 'If anyone shall say that grace is not conferred *ex opere operato*, but that belief in the Divine promise alone suffices to obtain grace, let him be anathema'.[11]

Because of the obvious dangers of a magical and superstitious use of baptism many Catholic theologians have much modified this view in the direction of the Reformed view while still seeking to retain the emphasis that the grace is conferred by virtue of the action of the Saviour God rather than by any virtue of the recipient's merit. We noted earlier that faith should not be understood as a meritorious action or attitude which offers a basis for deserving or even enabling the grace of God to operate.

Nevertheless this view does not do justice to the careful biblical balance between the effective sign and the context of faith. We have seen that the blessings of baptism are equally and indissolubly the blessings accorded to those who believe. Some are saved without baptism (the thief on the cross perhaps, among the Society of Friends and Salvation Army today); some are saved before baptism (Cornelius received the Spirit-baptism before the water-baptism); and some are not saved although they have been through baptism (as Paul warns in 1 Corinthians 10). As has been said, many of those inside (the church) are outside; and some of those outside are inside.[12]

Secondly, this view does not do justice to the biblical contrast between the outward and the inward. The outward sign is a precious covenant-sign from God and is not to be in any way despised. But it is not identical with what it signifies — unconditionally. So Paul writes 'A man is not a Jew if he is only one outwardly, nor is circumcision merely outward and physical. No, a man is a Jew if he is one inwardly; and circumcision is circumcision of the heart, by the Spirit, not by the written code' (Romans 2.28f).

Thirdly, while Paul speaks equally of baptism-blessings and faith-blessings, they are ultimately grace-blessings that come through the gospel of the Lord Jesus Christ. While as bold as any in using the sacramental language of baptismal efficacy, when Paul is faced with the divisions in the church at Corinth, and the horrendous speculation that anyone could possibly be a follower of, or baptized into, himself, Paul asserts strongly that he, personally, rarely performed baptism 'for Christ did not send me to baptize, but to preach the gospel' of the cross of Christ (1 Corinthians 1.15–17). While fully acknowledging that Paul is here responding sharply to a scandalous situation, and that baptism is a confirming sign of that very gospel of Christ crucified, nevertheless, Paul is pointing out that, in the last analysis, it is the word of the gospel received by faith that is the absolute priority. Without that context the sacrament, the covenant sign, loses its significance and power. 'Faith comes by hearing, and hearing by the word of God' (Romans 10.17).

The judgement in the Gorham controversy (1850) stated 'That Baptism is a sacrament generally necessary to salvation, but that the grace of regeneration does not so necessarily accompany the act of Baptism that regeneration invariably takes place in Baptism; that the grace may be granted before, in or after Baptism; that Baptism is an effectual sign of grace, by which God works invisibly in us, but only in such as worthily receive it — in them alone it has a wholesome effect; and that without reference to the qualification of the recipient it is not in itself an effectual sign of grace . . . that in no case is Baptism unconditional'.[13]

The *ex opere operato* view, then, does not fully meet the balance of the biblical teaching. It does not recognize sufficiently the covenant-context of proclamation of the divine promise in the gospel, and the necessity of a faith-response. The power of the covenant-sign is entirely from God as is the covenant gospel itself, but it must be accepted. It is not unconditional. Faith does not *make* the grace, but faith must *take* it.

3. *Baptism is desirable as a symbol of the blessings but does not convey them*. This view has been held to safeguard the essential condition of faith as the only and necessary way to receive God's offer of forgiveness and salvation. Baptism is certainly a symbol of salvation, but no integral link is seen between the symbol and the reality symbolized in terms of any effectual nature of the symbol.

This view is often described as 'Zwinglian' (after Zwingli, the Swiss Reformer 1484–1531) or 'Baptist'. The latter description, however, is unfortunate. Although very many 'baptist' churches (including probably the majority of Pentecostal, Brethren, Independent Evangelical and Restorationist 'House' churches) do teach this view, there are an increasing number of baptist theologians who have moved towards a sacramental view which is much closer to the 'Reformed', even though they still consider baptism of infants either improper or irregular.

Baptism is generally seen as proper and significant for the confessing believer for the following reasons:

(a) it is a step of obedience to Christ's direct command, and, therefore, part of discipleship;

(b) it was the normal practice of the early church as seen in the New Testament, and was used by the apostolic writers as a basis for their appeal to living in Christ, in holiness and in unity;
(c) it is a picture and symbol of the meaning of the gospel. This is seen in its identification with Jesus. Most (though not all) proponents of this view use immersion as the normal mode of baptism, and see its symbolism of burial and resurrection as the most significant characteristic of baptism;
(d) it is an opportunity (even *the* decisive opportunity) to witness to one's faith in Christ, to confess the faith in the waters of baptism. It is also an act of identification with the Christian community. However, many of the churches which take this view of baptism, either do not require baptism for, or do not closely link baptism with, church membership and/or Holy Communion.

Those who take this view of baptism usually place their whole emphasis on the preaching of the gospel of salvation. This must be received by faith and conversion. The born-again believer is then summoned to bear witness to his faith and conversion by the act of obedience in baptism. These churches are often marked paradoxically by a high degree of personal commitment to Christ along with a rather loose and voluntary view of church membership, and even, sometimes, of baptism itself.

The emphasis on receiving the gospel with an understanding faith was a vigorous reaction to the late medieval views in the Catholic Church which seemed to have an almost magical view of the sacraments allied to widespread carelessness about preaching the gospel of God's grace and summoning people to lives of trusting obedience. In this reaction, the 'missionary' adult baptisms of the Acts of the

Apostles were taken as the model. Unlike other Protestant Reformers they denied validity (as well as any kind of efficacy) to infant baptism. Upon a profession of faith, people who had been through a baptismal rite in infancy were 'baptized again'. This is why they gained the title 'Anabaptists', the re-baptizers. It is important to realize that those conscientiously holding this view do not agree with, and are aggrieved by, these terms 'Anabaptist' and 're-baptism'. On their understanding, it is not 'another baptism'; since infant baptism is theologically improper and invalid, it is only 'believer's baptism' which is true and valid baptism at all. This question of 're-baptism' will be examined more carefully in chapter 10.

However, there are some serious weaknesses in this view in the light of the whole of the biblical testimony:

First, it interprets the frequent passages which indicate the efficacy of baptism in a 'spiritual' sense, so that instead of referring to the outward sign they refer to the inward and spiritual reality that is signified. This results constantly in tautology, senseless repetition. For example when Paul says 'baptized into his death', it is interpreted as 'converted, born again into, sharing the significance of the death of Jesus of which water-baptism is a picture' (Romans 6.3). When Peter says 'Baptism now saves you', it is interpreted as 'conversion (being saved) now saves you, of which the water-ceremony is a witness and symbol' (1 Peter 3.21). But this is not what the passages say, and the exegesis becomes tortuous and artificial. Certainly the language of baptism-efficacy must always be interpreted in its unfailing context of faith in the gospel. Nevertheless the apostolic writers appear to have a much more dynamic understanding of the nature of the sacraments than those who take this view.

This is because, secondly, this theology effectively

associates baptism much more closely with the human response than with the divine promise, gift and sign. Proponents of this view draw a sharp contrast between the old covenant and its rite of circumcision and the new covenant in Christ and its rite of baptism in the name of Christ. The discontinuities are emphasized and the continuities interpreted in terms of spiritual typology. The sacraments, then, are seen not so much as God's covenant signs but rather as tokens and symbols of discipleship and Christian commitment. One popular and typical book representing this view[14] has a major section called 'Baptism and its meaning'. Its significance is summarized as — 'In baptism we actively and openly make declaration of certain facts'. These are fivefold — obeying, owning, dedication to, identification with and continuing with Jesus Christ. Now this is all true and implicit in baptism, but the New Testament writers say much more about God owning us in baptism, dedicating himself to us, and having identified himself with us *he* now identifies us with himself. *He* puts us into Christ, into his death and resurrection; *he* anoints us with the Spirit, and washes us with rebirth. In the New Testament, baptism, like the salvation it signifies, is Christo-centric, God-initiated, and Spirit-endowed. It loses so much of its rich and powerful assurance when not interpreted in its covenant-contexts. It must certainly have its faith context too, but the apostolic writers even saw believing faith as ultimately 'the gift of God' (Ephesians 2.8; cf. Philippians 1.29; Acts 18.27).

Finally, the heavy emphasis on witness to others in baptism is not according to the balance of New Testament teaching. Certainly, baptism may be a fine and effective witness to one's faith, and testimony to believers and unbelievers alike. But the apostolic writers do not make the point, let alone emphasize it. Rather, they expound baptism as primarily God's witness to us, his confirming sign of his covenant promise, the dramatic portrayal of his salvation and of the seal of his gift of the Spirit. The convert's witness emphasis is not biblical and, when taken out of the biblical covenant context, it is in grave danger of making baptism (and even salvation itself) man-centred. It is often too close to Pelaganianism for comfort.

This view is diametrically opposed to the *ex opere operato* interpretation, but like that, it fails to maintain the biblical covenant balance between word and action, promise and sign, outward ceremony and inward reality.

4. *The ceremony of water-baptism is unnecessary — it has no effect — but Spirit-baptism is its fulfilment*. Why bother with an outward symbol with water when one is daily enjoying the experienced reality with the Spirit? Outward forms become outmoded in the development of living realities.

This view is described as the 'Quaker' or 'Spirit-baptism' doctrine. The Society of Friends (the proper name for Quakers) are not so much opposed to water-baptism as indifferent to it. They say it is irrelevant because they continually seek to practise 'a sacramental life through the living presence of Christ'.[15]

The Salvation Army do not use the sacraments of baptism and holy communion either, but here it was originally due to their desire to be an evangelistic and mission agency rather than another church or denomination. There are other groups with a particular charismatic and Pentecostal emphasis who omit water-baptism in favour of the practice of Spirit baptism. Such groups are not a large proportion of world Christianity, but even amongst the major Confessions which practise baptism, there will frequently be found an undervaluing or misuse of it which virtually amounts to neglect or anti-sacrament-ism.

Like the development of the Zwinglian view, this doctrine of Spirit-baptism emerges as a strong reaction against a sacramentalism which appears to give all its emphasis to outward forms and ceremonies, formal orthodoxy and such doctrinal and legal scholasticisms as efficacy and validity.

It is urged that there is a strong contrast between baptism-with-water and Jesus' promise of baptism with-Spirit. Pentecost ushers in the new era of the Spirit, and the direct personal experience of his power and illumination seen in fruit of character and gifts of service renders the outward ceremonies redundant. Furthermore, it has been, and is, patently clear that God's grace and saving power cannot be confined to channels whether ecclesiastical, ministerial or sacramental. God's Spirit blows where it wills. People enter God's kingdom without baptism, and receive the baptism of Spirit without benefit of water-baptism. God's salvation is supremely a spiritual matter of grace and faith. Signs and ceremonies quite clearly are ineffective in certain situations, and where there is spiritual reality it is not because of the signs but because of the grace, faith and Spirit signified.

This can be presented as a very effective case. Any Christian should warm to an emphasis on spiritual realities as opposed to outward ceremonies and forms. There is a widespread feeling that ecclesiastical hierarchies and sacramental restrictions and formalities have 'quenched the Spirit'.

However, this view is far from the overall testimony of the New Testament writers. They see the closest relation between outward sign and spiritual reality, between water and Spirit, between Old Testament and New. Certainly the church and ministry must be continually alerted to the dangers of constraining and quenching the Spirit, but the covenant-signs and sacraments are regarded as 'means of grace' whereby God's promises are confirmed, clarified and conferred — in the context of faith. In spite of the contrast between water and Spirit, water-baptism was undergone by Jesus, commanded by him and consistently practised by the early church. The references to baptism in the Epistles cannot systematically be interpreted as Spirit-baptism — the water symbolism cannot be ignored. The examples of people spiritually alive apart from baptism, and spiritually dead with it can be acknowledged. There are exceptional situations on the one hand, and there is the necessity of faith-response on the other. This view, however, ignores the unity of the rich covenant scheme running throughout the Scripture with its pattern of promise and sign, word and confirming action. It misses a source of assurance and strength. It is always in danger of losing touch with the historical, the objective and the corporate dimensions of the sacraments in favour of the mystical, the subjective and the individualistic aspects. The Scriptural testimony unites the water-baptism and the Spirit-baptism in positive and creative harmony — the covenant sign and the covenant seal in God's saving purpose, both to be received by faith and worked out in a separated life of holiness. The sign of washing and seal of the Spirit belong together — 'Repent and be baptized and you will receive the forgiveness of sins, and the gift of the Holy Spirit' (Acts 2.38)

The biblical theology of Christian baptism is an immensely rich mine as it draws together the whole of God's eternal covenant plan of salvation with the simple yet profound and varied symbolism of water-washing. As with other Christian doctrines, the *whole* biblical material must be studied and in its contexts. The blessings of baptism embrace the entire gospel of God's grace, but it can only be known in the context of the covenant-pattern and in the context of the word of the gospel received by faith. *Efficacy there is* — as a sacrament, a covenant-sign from God, it is a gift of loving grace; *unconditional it is not* — as a sacrament, a covenant-sign from God, it is to be received with faith. 'Baptism is the divinely appointed rendezvous of grace for faith.'[16]

7

The Christian family

We have established the biblical theology of baptism as a covenant-sign (or sacrament) of God's grace, which is to be received in faith, and is used as a continual motivation for a life of holiness or separation to God. The New Testament writers clearly expect adult believers in Christ to be baptized. In the early years of the Church, delay in baptism seems to have been unknown, so that it is all who have been baptized who are 'in Christ', 'clothed with Christ', washed, adopted, recipients of the Holy Spirit and members of the Church, the body of Christ. Later in the history of the Church, as in many countries in this century, reasons for postponement (for teaching or testing, or through persecution and social factors) appeared convincing, but the apostolic writers seem not to envisage this in their teaching. The baptized are the Christians; the Christians are the baptized.

We turn now to the question of the children of believers, children of the Christian family. On the basis of the biblical theology of baptism, is there any justification for the covenant-sign of baptism being given to infants? On this issue there has been long and sad division in the Christian Church. This division has been exacerbated by a failure to hear properly what is the *best* case of the other side, and also a frequent appeal to inadequate theology and inadequate authority for that theology.

The polarization we have already noted appears again strongly. Those with a predominantly 'catholic' viewpoint strongly defend infant baptism, but very frequently on the basis of church tradition, or selective texts of Scripture. Those with a predominantly 'baptist' view deny the propriety of infant baptism at all — urging that infants cannot exercise repentance and faith, but they usually look to the Acts of the Apostles and selective texts in the Epistles without an awareness of the covenant contexts. This polarization has been seriously debilitating to Christian theology and mission. In the previous chapter we argued that the 'Reformed' or Covenant view most fully embraces the total biblical teaching on God's covenant-sign of baptism. However, very sadly, the application of this view to the question of household and infant baptism has frequently been spoiled by the development of alternative theologies of adult and infant baptism or the appeal to biblical texts that cannot bear the weight of the superstructures built upon them. It is of the greatest importance to the development of biblical and ecumenical theology that these inadequate approaches be avoided. The references to infant baptism in the WCC Report *Baptism, Eucharist and Ministry* are seriously inadequate at this point, and, by themselves, could do more harm than good.

Inadequate approaches to infant baptism

It would be the task of a major research (and very tedious) to detail the range of inadequate approaches. However, they must be examined in broad outline because of their damaging consequences both for practical pastoral work and inter-church relationships and discipline.

1. *An inadequate theology* of baptism is adopted by some proponents of infant baptism. We have seen that a biblical theology of baptism must hold together both the language of efficacy of God's covenant-sign of his grace and the necessity of the faith response. Time and again, theologians have sought to justify infant baptism by seriously reducing the significance

and reality of one or other of these two dimensions with regard to an infant.

On the one hand many Reformed theologians of an Evangelical standpoint have largely evacuated the full significance of efficacy-language in the case of infants, and spoken rather of 'the language of potential' or 'hypothetical' language. Where this is an alternative theology to that of adult or believer's baptism it is quite unacceptable from the standpoint of biblical theology. Quite simply there is no biblical support for two theologies of baptism — one adult, one infant.

On the other hand, many Reformed theologians on the more 'Catholic' side have seriously undervalued the significance and requirement of faith — both in the infant and in the family. Such a lack of nurture in faith, and practice of virtually indiscriminate infant baptism is strongly criticized in *BEM* IV C 16 and will be considered in detail in chapter 9. Where an alternative view of a 'seed' of faith or a 'potential' or 'hypothetical' faith is developed without a context of a living faith and nurture of faith, this view is again seriously unacceptable in the light of the biblical theology. Without faith, we cannot please God, and his covenant sign of grace must always be met by a living faith.

2. *An inadequate authority* frequently underlies an inadequate theology, or sometimes good conclusions are based upon weak and inadequate arguments. Bad arguments added to good ones do not offer further support, they simply undermine the good arguments and impair the development of biblical theology. Bad support for a good biblical position undermines and discredits the theology. Too often the case for infant baptism has been based on early church tradition, and this is the sole basis offered in *BEM* Section IV A. Those of Reformed tradition often complacently refer

back to the Protestant Reformers of the 16th century, to Luther and Calvin, to the Anglican 39 Articles and Presbyterian Westminister Confession. But this will not do in biblical or ecumenical theology. An appeal to church tradition can only be supportive of, and must never be regarded as foundational and constitutive of, Christian doctrine.

Another form of arguing from inadequate authority has been the use of select biblical passages to bear the weight of a theological superstructure that they cannot securely support. The following passages may well be agreeable to the baptism of infants but by themselves they cannot be held to *require* it. Such passages are, for example, Mark 10.14 Jesus said, 'Let the little children come to me, and do not hinder them'; the oikos 'household' formula used repeatedly in the 'Acts' and in 1 Corinthians 1.16; the holiness of a child of a believing parent, 1 Corinthians 7.14; and finally, the parallel drawn between baptism and circumcision in Colossians 2.11f. All these are significant passages which will be examined later. However, they simply do not, as such, demonstrate the propriety of baptizing infants, and it is futile to imagine or to argue that they do. Such arguments have, over the years, lulled paedo-baptists into a quite false sense of theological security, and caused those of baptist conviction to suspect the biblical and theological integrity of the paedo-baptist case. It is one of the greatest tragedies of the history of Christian doctrine that so many theological debates have been conducted, not only with acrimony, but on the basis of an inadequate authority and with careless attention to biblical exegesis, and the full context.

The biblical case for Christian family baptism

The apostolic writers of the New Testament give us no explicit and unambiguous evidence about the baptism of the children of the Christian family. There is no explicit account or teaching of an infant baptism, but neither is there any account or teaching of the adult baptism of a child born into a Christian family. So the case is not a matter of unambiguous biblical precedent or instruction. This should immediately warn all engaged in the debate to be cautious, careful and respectful to other carefully presented positions.

As with other issues where there is no explicit biblical command or example, biblical theology proceeds on the basis of legitimate inference. It will be a matter of judgement how strongly or otherwise the general weight of the biblical theology renders such an inference, but it will be a matter of the *general pattern* of biblical theology and *not* a matter of looking for proof-texts that settle the issue one way or the other. The classic example of legitimate inference with no direct biblical command or example is the matter of women sharing in Holy Communion. Most Christians are quite unembarrassed by the lack of explicit evidence but regard the issue as settled by the general New Testament teaching about the unity of the Body of Christ and the lack of any instruction to the contrary. But an appeal to proof texts would be a very dangerous expedient in this case. It would be a very tempting short-cut to appeal to Paul's great claim that 'there is neither male nor female, for you are all one in Christ Jesus' (Galatians 3.28). But it *would* be a short-cut, for the passage is not speaking about Holy Communion explicitly. If it is used as a proof text for women at Communion it would equally *prove* the rightness of the ordination of women. The point is, that with respect to many matters of church life we do, and can only, work on this basis of legitimate inference rather than direct instruction. In passing, we might add that even apparently direct instruction will need to be carefully interpreted in the light of its historical and literary contexts. Thus there is no need for embarrassment at this point — whatever conclusion we may feel the biblical theology points to in the end. The question we ask is: in the light of the general teaching of the Bible, and more especially the New Testament, is it more agreeable to the apostolic witness to bring the infants of Christians to baptism or not?

There are three main lines of evidence:

the covenant principle
the family principle
the sacramental principle

We immediately agree that none of these matters is explicitly baptismal, but remind the reader that there is *no* incontrovertible evidence one way or the other on the specific issue of the baptism of infants of a Christian family. In each case we shall examine the general biblical theology and then look at certain passages in the New Testament and ask whether or not they make better sense if the apostolic writers were assuming Christian family baptism. Much of the evidence has already been expounded in previous chapters, and so in order to prevent tedious repetition there will inevitably be references back to those passages.

1. *The Covenant principle* as a recurring biblical pattern was followed through the Scriptures in chapter 3. We noted that the marks of this covenant principle included the primacy and initiative of God's grace, the supreme spiritual blessing 'I will be your God and you will be my people', the necessity of receiving God's covenant promise with faith that issues in obedience, the use of covenant signs which signify, seal and embody God's covenant grace, and the pattern of promise and fulfilment. We noted the continuity of the essential elements of this covenant

pattern in the 'new covenant' — especially in terms of the initiative of grace and the necessity of responding faith.

In chapter 2 we considered each of the references to baptism in the New Testament epistles and discovered that the apostolic writers naturally and regularly thought of baptism in terms of covenant situations, covenant imagery, covenant blessings and covenant response. The use in these passages of Abraham, Moses and Noah is remarkable. It is in the light of this great pattern of biblical theology that the parallel of circumcision and baptism in Colossians 2.11f must be interpreted. In view of Paul's baptismal and eucharistic language applied to the Israelites in 1 Corinthians 10, it is not in the least surprising that he asserts that the same spiritual realities are signified in circumcision and baptism (see p. 21). There is no proof of infant baptism here, but the inference seems clear. It is against this background, and in this context that the crowd heard Peter preach 'The promise (rich covenant word) is for you and for your children and to all that are afar off' (Acts 2.39). No proof again, but yet another indication of the covenant principle.

2. *The family principle* is closely associated with the covenant pattern. God's initiative of grace has a special emphasis on the family unit. While each individual stands responsible before God for disobedience and unfaithfulness to the covenant, nevertheless, there is a strong element of family solidarity running through the Scriptures. Noah was called to take his whole family with him into the ark, the promise to Abraham was also to his descendants after him. Yet we have noted that God's covenant promises were not merely racial, tribal or national. From the beginning there was a universal dimension, and from the beginning the enjoyment of covenant grace by each person was by faith.

Paul writes about the solidarity of the Israelites who were baptized 'into Moses in the cloud and in the sea'. This baptism was in no way automatic in its benefits or unconditional with respect to faith and obedience. For 'with many of them God was not pleased' and they forfeited the enjoyment of salvation. The rebellion of Korah (Numbers 16) and the dishonesty of Achan (Joshua 7) are further examples of the solidarity of the family household. (See also Deuteronomy 29.10–12) Psalm 103.17f; Isaiah 65.23; Jeremiah 32.38–41.)

When the Jews later adopted baptism for the initiation of Gentile converts or proselytes to be 'children of the covenant' it is not surprising that they baptized the adult converts and the children of the family too. It does not matter about the exact date of the introduction of this practice, although it seems to have been established before the baptizing ministry of John, the point is that when the Judaic leaders admitted converts they considered the family, especially the small children, would join too. The family principle was an integral and natural part of their thought patterns with respect to conversion and the covenant people of God.

It is against this background that we now examine New Testament references to families and little children. Detailed exegesis of these passages will not be attempted nor the baptist objections to the use of them. None of these passages by themselves demonstrate or require infant baptism (as already made clear on p. 106). However, the reader is asked to judge whether or not they are better interpreted in the light of the biblical tradition of the family principle.

(a) children were addressed as members of the church — 'children obey your parents *in the Lord*' (Ephesians 6.1; Colossians 3.20; 1 John 2.13 — although John often uses the term 'children' metaphorically, here it is likely to be literal). The significance of children growing up 'in the Lord' can scarcely be exaggerated for the phrase is baptismal, and enshrines all the blessings of the covenant and salvation. This reminds us of the angel's prophecy to Zechariah about John 'He will be filled with the Holy Spirit even from birth' (literally 'from his mother's womb' Luke 1.15)

(b) there are several references to *'the household'* in connection with baptism, — with Lydia, with the jailer of Philippi, and with Stephanas (Acts 16.15; 16.33; 1 Corinthians 1.16), and probably with Cornelius (Acts 10.48, cf. 11.14). See also Crispus (Acts 18.8). There is no *proof* that these households contained infants, though perhaps in the context of an extended family pattern it is highly likely. It is the family principle clearly in operation once again. (See also Luke 19.9.)

(c) 'the *promise* is for you and *your children'* (Acts 2.39) said Peter. He goes on to speak of its universal relevance and application, just as God had earlier in the covenant proclamation to Abraham: 'All nations will be blessed', but within that universal plan is the family principle.

(d) the difficult passage in 1 Corinthians 7.14 is about an unbelieving partner being sanctified by the believing partner who has been converted after marriage 'otherwise *your children* would be unclean, but as it is, *they are holy'*. It seems best to interpret this passage in the light of covenant 'separation' and family solidarity. It is unlikely to refer to civil legitimacy, nor is it likely to mean moral holiness of character. The words 'unclean' and 'holy' are covenant status words, which speak first of God's consecration of things or people, and then of their subsequent life of moral and spiritual separtion to God's service. The unbelieving partner must embrace the gospel by faith in order to be saved (7.16), and the children must grow up 'in the Lord' to make this holy status a living reality of faith and obedience. But, in the mercy of God, the conversion of a parent draws the whole family into the covenant privileges (and responsibilities) of God.

(e) *Jesus' attitude* to little children is quite striking. 'If anyone causes one of these little ones who believe in me to sin, it would be better for him to have a large millstone hung around his neck and to be drowned in the depths of the sea' (Matthew 18.6). Jesus said 'Let the little children come to me, and do not hinder them, for the kingdom of heaven belongs to such as these'. He placed his hands on them with his blessing (Matthew 19.13f). In the parallel passage at Mark 10.13f there is the addition 'I tell you the truth, anyone who will not receive the kingdom of God like a little child will never enter it'. Little children can believe, and be led astray, they can be brought to Jesus and be members of the kingdom (under the rule) of God, and their simple trustfulness is an example to all.

None of these passages are *proof* texts for infant baptism, but, when understood in the covenant context, they provide grounds for a legitimate inference that is a matter of biblical and spiritual integrity and not just a case of special pleading.

3. *The Sacramental principle* has been explored in the previous chapter (p. 81). The sacrament is an action or sign which confirms God's word of promise. It speaks of the saving work of Almighty God, — the electing love of the Father, the reconciling sacrifice of the Son, and the regenerating power of the Spirit. Sacraments are God's gifts to us, rather than things we do for him. They are signs of grace rather than witness to faith. However, they must be received with faith.

God's grace is secure and his promise utterly

dependable, but although faith is a gift of God it is worked out in human response, and this response is not always easy to evaluate. When an adult confesses repentance, faith and conversion, some church leaders will offer baptism immediately (as seems the practice in the earliest days of the church). Other leaders, however, will offer further instruction, make further enquiry into the reality of the faith and test it in various ways. Quite often someone baptized as an adult will appear to fall away from faith. Similarly, with the child of a Christian family, the response may be erratic, complex, sometimes inconsistent or even hostile.

However, in spite of these inevitable uncertainties (which are paralleled in adults), it appears appropriate:

(a) to bring up children of a Christian family *in the grace of God*. Thus, we teach them to know and pray to God as Father (1 John 2.13), and, therefore, to consider themselves his children, to know Jesus as friend and saviour from sin, to ask forgiveness for wrong, to seek God's strength (i.e. from the Spirit) to do what is right, to live a godly life 'in the Lord' rather than a selfish life 'of the world', to experience the church as the family of God. These are the full blessings of the gospel, of salvation, of the covenant, of baptism and of faith in God's promises.

(b) to bring up children of a Christian family *in repentance, faith and obedience to God*. Thus, we teach them the law of God, right and wrong, to confess their sin and trust God's offer of forgiveness, and to grow in grace and in the knowledge of the Lord Jesus. These things come long before intellectual comprehension or years of discretion. They can become part of an infant's experience along with the love, care and protection of parents, and growing awareness of others from whom one receives love and care, and to whom one should offer love and respect.

(c) to offer such a child *the covenant-sign, or sacrament, of God's grace in baptism*. Baptism is initiation into Christian life. But the deepest concern and most earnest prayer of every Christian parent should be that from the very beginning of life, the child will live God's new life 'in the Lord' and so grow in grace and in the Spirit of God. What grounds are there for making knowledge of, and love for, God a matter of intellectual understanding and some hypothetical age of discretion, when no such criterion could be applied to knowledge of, and love for, a mother and father? Baptism marks the beginning (not a further stage) of discipleship to Jesus. It should then be worked out, whether in adult convert or Christian child, in a baptized life — cleansed, in Christ, through the Spirit, child of God, member of the church. Baptism has past, present and future dimensions with respect to God's covenant plan of grace; it also has past, present and future dimensions with respect to the faith response.

Issues related to infant baptism

We shall now consider four related issues arising from the consideration of the propriety of baptizing the children of Christian parents. These are:

the issue of indiscriminate baptism
the liturgical language in the services of baptism
the question why baptism replaced circumcision
the question whether the salvation of infants depends on baptism

There are many thoughtful Christians who will follow the biblical argument up to this point, but for whom the issues of indiscriminate baptism and the liturgical language are highly significant obstacles. This is well understood and the topics require careful attention.

1. *The issue of indiscriminate baptism* is deeply distressing to many Christians, and the major reason why many of baptist conviction are doubtful of the theological integrity of those who defend Christian family baptism. Indiscriminate baptism of infants occurs primarily in countries which have established or state churches and where, over the centuries, there have been close links with or even identity between church and state. In these situations the baptism of infants becomes a social or cultural norm or custom, and there may be little or no understanding of the gospel, little or no credible confession of faith, membership of the church or likelihood of real Christian nurture. In terms of the theology of Christian baptism that has been developed in these chapters such a ceremony can be seen more as a rite of folk religion than 'christening' or being baptized into Christ. The pressure of this folk religion is historically deep-seated and profoundly subtle, but the *BEM* document asserted vigorously that those who practise infant baptism 'must guard themselves against the practice of apparently indiscriminate baptism and take more seriously their responsibility for the nurture of baptized children to mature commitment to Christ'.[1]

The issue of a proper discipline over infant baptism which fully preserves the context of living faith in the gospel of Jesus will be examined in chapter 9. Suffice to say at this moment, that the biblical theology of infant baptism can only be argued with integrity in the context of a proper discipline of practice. Even where the biblical theology of infant baptism is not inadequate, the pastoral practice can leave much to be desired. This, however, can be a problem in baptist churches too. Faulty practice must make us ask searching questions about the theology behind such practice. However, if we are satisfied about the legitimate inference of the propriety of Christian family baptism, it is the faulty pastoral practice that needs reform and not the biblical theology of covenant sign and sacrament.

2. *The liturgical language in the services of baptism* causes widespread embarrassment and misunderstanding. The old Book of Common Prayer (1662) states after the baptism

> 'seeing now that this child is regenerate and grafted into the body of Christ's Church, let us give thanks unto Almighty God for these benefits, and with one accord make our prayers unto him . . . We yield Thee hearty thanks, most merciful father, that it hath pleased Thee to regenerate this infant with Thy Holy Spirit, to receive him for Thine own by adoption, and to incorporate him into Thy holy Church.'

Similarly the Church of England Alternative Service Book (1980) says:

> God has received you by baptism into his Church.
> We welcome you into the Lord's family.
> We are members together of the body of Christ;
> we are children of the same heavenly Father;
> we are inheritors together of the Kingdom of God.
> We welcome you.
> Lord God our Father . . . we thank you that by your Holy Spirit these children have been born again into new life, adopted for your own, and received into the fellowship of your Church.

Sincere Christians are hostile to, or at least uneasy about, such expressions. They often feel that when applied to an infant, they undermine the New Testament emphasis on the necessity of faith. A similar problem could be felt with regard to an adult baptism candidate for we cannot be *totally sure* that the fruit of spiritual regeneration will mature following an initial profession of faith. However, we *assume* the sincerity of the profession of repentance and faith, and, in addition may *require* some evidence in terms of instruction received and sharing in church life. On some such basis, we speak of the baptized person in terms of all the realities which baptism signifies — born again, a child of God etc.

Similarly, in the case of the Christian household baptism of an infant, we cannot be *totally sure* that the fruit of spiritual regeneration will mature following nurture in the faith of Christ. However, we *assume* the grace of God at work in terms of the covenant and family principles, and the sincerity of the parents' promises to bring up the child in the Lord and in faith, and, in addition, may *require* some evidence on the part of the parents in terms of instruction received and sharing in church life. On this basis, we speak of the baptized child in terms of all the realities which baptism signifies — born again, a child of God and so on.

This is the language of baptismal efficacy the New Testament writers use — but it is always *faith* language. It is not unconditional efficacy. For the language of covenant and sacrament always requires the context of faith. So the BCP continues after the thanksgiving quoted above

> And humbly we beseech thee to grant that he being dead unto sin, and living unto righteousness, and being buried with Christ in his death, may crucify the old man, and utterly abolish the whole body of sin; and that, as he is made partaker of the death of thy Son, he may be partaker of his resurrection; so that finally, with the residue of thy holy Church, he may be an inheritor of thine everlasting kingdom.

and the ASB continues after its thanksgiving quoted above:—

> grant that they may grow in the faith
> into which they have been baptized,
> that they may profess it for themselves
> when they come to be confirmed,
> and that all things belonging to the Spirit
> may live and grow in them

This language of expectant faith is categorical in form (i.e. describing the sign in terms of the realities signified) but it is hypothetical or conditional in effect (i.e. it depends on the living response of faith). It is intriguing to remember that the Anglican Reformers who are sometimes criticized for underplaying faith in their baptism liturgy actually died at the stake for the principle of justification by faith in their communion liturgy. The baptism liturgies of the Church of England are designed to express the two New Testament factors of baptism — the efficacy of the covenant sign of God's grace and the necessity of its right reception with faith. The language of one factor must be seen and interpreted in the context of the other factor.

The use of language to speak of a reality which is categorical in one sense but conditional in another sense has parallels in other situations of daily life. Take the wedding ceremony, for example. The bride and groom make their vows, give and receive the ring, and are solemnly pronounced to be 'man and wife'. This *categorical* assertion is never questioned by the guests at the wedding, but it is in actual fact *conditional* on their consummating their marriage and living together as man and wife. If this expectation is unfulfilled, then, vows and ring notwithstanding, the marriage can be null and void. We cannot be *totally sure* it will be a proper marriage. However, we *assume* the sincerity of their professions of love and taking, and, in addition, may well have seen evidence in terms of instruction about marriage and sharing in courtship and engagement.

Another example is to be found in the handing over of a postal order. The postal order is made out for (let us say) a thousand pounds, with the recipient's name, and handed to him. We then regard the beneficiary as one thousand pounds better off. No one dreams of questioning the *categorical* assertion that the beneficiary has received one thousand pounds, but it is in actual fact *conditional* on his taking the postal order to a Post Office, signing his name and claiming the money. If this expectation is unfulfilled, and the postal order is forgotten, lost, or left in a drawer, the order's promise and payment notwithstanding, it fails to benefit the recipient. We cannot be *totally sure* the postal order will be used. However, we *assume* the grateful acceptance and use of the gift on the part of the recipient, and, in addition, may have some evidence in terms of his knowledge about postal orders and use of the Post Office.

The ring and the postal order have no inherent value for marriage or wealth in and of themselves — their full significance is conditional on the context and subsequent action. So, with baptism, the gift of God's grace to adult or infant — the full significance is conditional on the context of faith and the subsequent action of a life of faith.

The liturgical language, similarly, is *categorical* in form (expressing the biblical teaching of the efficacy of baptism), but it is *conditional* in effect (requiring the response of faith for its full effect). This language is the Scriptural language of covenant sign and sacrament. It expresses the totality of the covenant promise as well as the necessity of the faith response. The assertions of efficacy are a matter for joy and encouragement in the assurance of God's initiative of grace; while the petition for growth in Christian life is a matter for earnest prayer, faith, and dedicated nurture. The dimunition of either factor would impair the liturgical expression of the biblical doctrine.

3. *The question why baptism replaced circumcision* has not yet been answered in this enquiry. The New Testament writers seem to *assume* the priority of baptism as Christian initiation, and Jesus' words in the Great Commission, Matthew 28.19, clearly express the convictions of the early Christians. The first Jewish Christians did not immediately and obviously detach themselves from Judaism, its customs and ceremonies. They continued to attend Temple and synagogue and to use the covenant sign of circumcision alongside the new covenant sign of baptism. There are several factors that gradually led to the complete replacement of circumcision by baptism:

(a) the increasing *hostility of Jews* against Christianity led to even Jewish Christians being expelled from synagogues and probably the Temple. The destruction of the Temple of Jerusalem in AD 70, and the rapid growth of the Christian movement among Gentiles altered the whole relationship in a radical fashion.

(b) the identification of circumcision with the *Jewish legalism* of justification by works meant that circumcision became a symbol of this errant religious approach (Acts 15.5; Galatians 5.2f; 6.12f). This is why Paul attacks the 'circumcision party' with such ferocity in letters to the Galatians and Philippians. It is not that circumcision rightly understood is anything other than God's covenant sign of his promise to Abraham and to all others who will follow him by faith, but the Jewish legalists had made it the first and essential requirement in a religious system of righteousness by good works — a system which denied the grace of God, the power of Christ's death on the cross, and the sole requirement of faith in Christ in order to be right with God.

(c) both the signs of the old covenant, circumcision and Passover, involved the *shedding of blood*. This reminded God's people that 'without the shedding of blood there is no forgiveness' of sins (Hebrews 9.22). However, the sacrificial death of Christ and the shedding of his blood has fulfilled all these signs. 'When this priest had offered for all time one sacrifice for sins, he sat down at the right hand of God' (Hebrews 10.12).

New covenant signs are now appropriate which do not involve the shedding of blood but which point back to the perfect sacrifice of Christ.

(d) in the light of the initiatory use of *baptism for proselytes and by John*, the simple and symbolic rite of water-washing was highly appropriate and available as the sign of entry to the new covenant in Christ.

(e) it has often been asserted that baptism is superior to circumcision as a covenant sign because it is offered *to women* as well as men. There might be some weight in this point, but perhaps many people misunderstand the full significance of circumcision in Old Testament faith. Unlike the surrounding nations its significance was not racial but religious, not linked with puberty but with covenant in infancy or at conversion. Although it is the male sex organ's fore-skin that is removed, in the sharing of married love and procreation there is the closest possibly sharing at that point between husband and wife. Surely there is significance in the fact that at the moment of supreme expression of sexual love and the essential moment of conception, the covenant sign of God's grace is at the centre, and shared in joyful solemnity by man and wife.

(f) finally, the *spiritual realities* symbolized in circumcision are fully symbolized in baptism — death to an old life, birth to a new life through God's gracious power.

4. *The question whether the salvation of infants depends on baptism* mustly surely be answered with a firm negative. We have seen that the blessings of salvation are all linked to baptism, and that the identical blessings are linked to receiving the gospel by faith. However, behind both these truths is the ultimate and primary truth that the blessings of salvation come from the grace of God, the God of grace, alone. Those who hold a baptist theology often dedicate their infants to God, give them to him and seek his blessing (of salvation) for them from the day of birth. Believers can entrust their infants (whether living or dying) to the mercy of God with utter confidence in his loving mercy and covenant grace. Then as they grow up, the children must *affirm* their desire to be in the Lord, converted to Christ, and thus *confirm* their baptism.

The biblical language of covenant-signs and the liturgical language of the sacraments is always the language of faith. Infant baptism has precisely the same theological significance as adult baptism. It is God's covenant sign of his saving grace. It effects what it signifies, not automatically, but within the context of living faith.

The basis for this conviction is founded on appeal to Scripture alone. Just as indiscriminate adult baptism would be a denial of the necessity of faith, so indiscriminate infant baptism is destructive of the true nature of the sacrament. That is why it is better termed 'Christian family baptism'. It must be emphasized again — there is only one theology of baptism, and that is believers' baptism. It is God's covenant sign to adult believers and to their children who are brought up in the grace and the faith of the Lord.

8

The 'baptist' view

Those who hold a 'baptist' view regard the case for Christian infant baptism expounded in the previous chapter as unconvincing. The title of this chapter is slightly misleading but avoids being pedantic. The fact is that there is no one 'baptist view'. Just as at the beginning of the previous chapter it was acknowledged that there have been various and inadequate expositions of infant baptism, so now we note that there are various views amongst those who disagree with infant baptism. It would be all too easy to quote copiously from quite unbiblical and incoherent passages of baptist writers and let them cancel out each other's positions. This approach has been repeatedly adopted against the family-baptism doctrine.[1] However, this is no way to conduct serious debate about biblical theology. It should be the *best* presentation of the opponents' case which is answered. Division about the defence of a theological position or the abuse resulting from such a position may properly form a part of theological debate, but the best answer to abuse may not be disuse but right use.

However, a major division amongst baptist scholars must be noted. Probably the majority still hold to the Zwinglian or 'symbolic' view of baptism which was examined in chapter 6 (p. 94). A growing number, though, recognize some of the biblical criticisms of that position and have adopted what is often called a 'sacramental' view, i.e. that baptism is a sign (and effective sign) of grace and not merely a symbol of faith in the gospel.

The general baptist view has been outlined earlier, but now we examine further:

Arguments against Christian family baptism

The first and major objection to infant baptism is:

1. *Baptism should follow faith and be an expression of faith*. All 'baptists' are agreed that baptism should follow a conscious profession of faith on the part of the candidate. They argue that this is the clear pattern of the Lord's Great Commission, in the accounts of the Acts of the Apostles, and that it is clearly implied in the Epistles. Baptism is an expression of the convert's faith, and a witness or testimony to it. An infant cannot make a decision to confess faith in the waters of baptism.

There is a major problem with this doctrinal position. The apostolic writers, as noted earlier, do *not* explain baptism as a witness to faith, but rather, as God's witness to his grace that is received in faith. This is a distinctly different approach. We saw earlier that V. Jack[2] explains the whole significance of baptism in terms of the convert confessing Christ, and in terms of the believer's response. Even Beasley-Murray, who holds a sacramental baptist view, writes[3] 'It is universally recognized that in the primitive Church baptism was the occasion par excellence for the confession of faith in Christ'. He then cites four texts (Acts 8.36ff; Romans 1.9; Ephesians 5.26; 1 Peter 3.18ff), none of which explicitly link baptism and witness, and concludes that they 'provide sufficient evidence on this point'.

Now as we said earlier, baptism of adult converts obviously involves a declaration of faith in Christ, but the New Testament writers nowhere speak of it in terms of witness to others — believers or unbelievers.

The crucial point is that the baptist doctrine puts the emphasis in the wrong place. Certainly baptism must be in the context of gospel proclamation received by faith, but essentially and primarily, the apostolic writers declare it to be God's covenant sign of *his grace*. This is the correct doctrine of all baptism — adult as well as infant. A child should only receive the sign if he/she is to be nurtured by parent or guardian in the Lord, in the knowledge of his grace and in trustful dependence on him. Baptism marks the initiation or beginning of Christian discipleship. For an adult convert, that will be at some point near his conversion, but for a child of Christian parents discipleship should, can and does start from the very commencement of life. This is God's ideal for the Christian family. Baptism *may* prove unfruitful — both in the professing adult convert and in the child of the Christian home. Nevertheless, when this occurs in an adult who is later genuinely converted to spiritual renewal, no responsible Baptist ministers offer a 'second' baptism. This is an example which indicates that the principle 'baptism must follow conscious faith' can have its exceptions, even among adults.

2. *Baptism does not convey salvation automatically*. This is entirely agreed. The *ex opere operato* view was criticized in chapter 6. It was there argued that the biblical doctrine combines both strong sacramental language of efficacy along with a clear emphasis on the necessity of faith response. God's covenant promise of grace and God's covenant sign which confirms that promise are not automatically enjoyed, or offered unconditionally — they must be received by faith. The same problem occurs with an adult as with the child of a Christian family. We can never be absolutely sure that the faith will develop and persist, but we presume the sincerity of the faith-context and that the right conditions for spiritual growth will continue. When Beasley-Murray criticises the explanation of infant baptism as a promise with a condition,[4] he says 'observe what a drastic change has been wrought in the nature of baptism so administered.

Baptism has been reduced from a sacrament to a sermon, from a gift to an offer, from an event of eternal consequence to an uncertain possibility'. But he protests too much! Unless we are to believe in an invariable baptismal regeneration in adult baptism (let alone infant) we are bound to acknowledge that the sacrament is an acted and confirmed *sermon* from God, a gift that is *offered* by God, and an event of eternal consequence which nevertheless has a real element of *uncertainty* in the sense that we can never presume on God's mercy and must ever emphasize the responsibility of responding with faith.

This is precisely why the Anglican liturgies combine the two distinct elements — the assertion of baptismal efficacy in terms of the gracious promise of God is sure, but there is also the heartfelt prayer that the candidates (adult and infant) will grow in the faith and show fruit worthy of repentance and life in Christ.

3. *Salvation and faith is an individual matter, not hereditary*. It is agreed, that in the final analysis every individual will stand before God responsible for his own attitudes and actions. This was true in Old Testament times as well as in the time of the new covenant in Christ. But there is also much evidence in both testaments, as we have seen (p. 108), for the family principle within God's covenant plan of grace. There are inestimable privileges in being brought up 'in the Lord' but there are equally great responsibilities. The child is not automatically saved irrespective of Christian nurture or the response of faith and commitment. Salvation and faith is not a matter of heredity.

Thus, we find that these three objections fail to show Christian infant baptism to be unbiblical. Firstly, baptism is primarily a covenant sign of God's grace given to his people at the very beginning of their life of discipleship. It is to be received and lived out by faith, but is not itself essentially a witness to faith. Secondly, baptism does not convey its blessings of salvation automatically either to adult or infant. The salvation is conditional upon the promises being truly received in living and continuing faith. Thirdly, salvation and faith are certainly not hereditary, in spite of the clear family principle in the Scriptures. A Christian family does bring great blessing but not automatically, and not by natural birth. The blessings of salvation are conditional upon living faith and new birth by the Spirit of God. But why should God not grant the miracle of new birth to the infant at physical birth so he can grow up 'in the Lord'?

We now move on to consider:

Problems of the baptist doctrine

These are considerable and not often recognized. It is usually baptists who are most interested in baptism and on the attack while most members of churches which practise infant baptism often know little theology of baptism and are insecure and defensive. Those who have sincerely followed the development of the biblical case for Christian family baptism need not feel their position is threatened by criticisms aimed at either inadequate arguments for infant baptism or of indiscriminate baptism. Neither are necessary and both are abuses of the biblical teaching. It is the best and biblical case for infant baptism and the proper administration of it in the truly believing family that must be answered.

There are three serious weakness of biblical theology in the baptist doctrine. The first two have been considered already in this chapter, (p. 123). They are —

1. Baptism is seen as a *symbol of faith* rather than as a sign of grace. This leads inevitably to a man-centred ceremony rather than a Christ-centred sacrament which is given by God and involves the seal of the Spirit. This is a serious distortion of the biblical doctrine which some baptist theologians are seeking to correct by developing a more sacramental theology.

2. Baptism is given an emphatic importance as *witness to others*. It may well be a powerful witness, especially when an adult is converted but this is not a significant part of apostolic doctrine. Witness to Christ is vital but is focussed on the continuing baptized life of holiness rather than the initial baptismal event (Rom 10.9). Once again, the perceived direction is wrong. Baptism is primarily not something a person does either for God or as a witness to others, it is something God gives to him. It is *God's* witness to his promise of saving grace. (See also chapter 6, p. 97). Then also —

3. Baptism is not acknowledged as essentially *a covenant-sign*. This is the fundamental weakness of biblical theology which underlies the first two problems. The essential covenant nature of the sacrament is not generally recognized by baptist theologians — the covenant language, imagery, contexts and illustrations so clearly seen in chapter 2 where we considered each baptism reference in the Epistles. This was the essential pattern of apostolic understanding, and failure to recognize it leads inevitably to a whole range of erroneous exegesis. The covenant continuity is seriously undervalued and the discontinuities exaggerated (as worked out at the end of chapter 3). This means that most baptist theologians gravely misjudge the nature of the covenant with Abraham and its developments with Moses and

David. Repeatedly it is described as outward (not inward), concerned with natural birth (not spiritual life), racially exclusive (not a universal promise) with circumcision a mere mark of the flesh (not a sign of spiritual grace). There is a serious confusion here between understanding God's gracious covenant intention and provisions, and the legalistic distortion of the promise and sign that developed from the misuse of the law as an attempted means of salvation.

Finally, there is a serious practical and pastoral problem —

4. *How to bring up a child in a Christian family*. Quite simply the question is this — should Christian parents bring up their children as 'in the Lord' and needing to grow in grace and in the knowledge of Christ, or assuming that they are outside of Christ and his kingdom and needing to be converted at some age of understanding? This is a very personal and sensitive matter and there is no desire to cause any offence. However, the baptist theology points to the latter of the two options, and both Davies[5] and Watson[6] are quite explicit that children of Christian families should be assumed to be unconverted until showing clear evidence to the contrary. In actual practice, many baptist parents *do* bring their children up as Christians in about the same way as parents who have baptized their children with the covenant sign. Many such children have never known a time when they did not trust God as Father, Jesus as Saviour and Friend and the Spirit as Guide and Strengthener. All speculation about ages of discretion or conscious understanding are subjective and fruitless. One might just as well ask when a child starts to love and trust her parents. It is a non-sense question which betrays an intellectual approach to a matter which is far more to do with 'infant-like' trust and emotional response of love than it is to mental under-

standing. We have noted that John was Spirit-filled from his birth. Timothy had from his childhood known the Scriptures which taught him of God's salvation. This is God's ideal for children — never to know a time outside God's kingdom, a stranger to God's love, without God's Spirit's power.

If Christian parents *do* believe God can bring spiritual life when he chooses (since all regeneration in adult or infant is a miracle of God's grace, and a new birth only God's Spirit can effect), at what point will they give the covenant sign of that grace? When the two year old says 'I love Jesus', or the three year old 'Our Father in heaven', or the four year old says 'Dear God, I'm sorry, please help me'? Such prayers cannot be lightly dismissed. Some baptists do offer 'believer's baptism' to children of five and upwards, but it is a hazardous pastoral matter assessing conscious faith at such an age.

However, if Christian parents do *not* believe God can bring new spiritual life until a child reaches an age when she is capable of a conscious and 'meaningful' profession of repentance, faith and conversion, they are in a very difficult position with regard to Christian nurture. Before the supposed time of possible conversion, the child will be under law rather than grace, and God will be Judge rather than Father, and Jesus will be Teacher rather than Friend. These problems of nurture indicate that something may be wrong with the premise. Surely it is biblically and pastorally more appropriate in a Christian Family to bring up our children in the Lord, in glad and confident awareness of his saving grace, and in trusting and obedient response which matures with the years. We must not expect an 'adult' faith in a two-year old — the response will be appropriate to the development.

The question may well be asked 'How, then, do we know if and when a child is regenerate?' Once again, the answer must be the same with regard to adult and infant. The answer is that we can never be totally sure (in the sense that $5 + 5 = 10$), but we can have a real *faith* in her regeneration on the basis of God's promise of grace and the context of faith. In the adult convert, God's promise has been given in the gospel and we presume the sincerity of the response of faith in the context of Christian nurture; in the child of a Christian family too, God's promise has been given in the gospel and we presume the sincerity of the response of faith in the context of Christian nurture. It is not automatic or hereditary or a matter of natural birth. It is conditional, spiritual and a matter of birth from above. Nevertheless, in baptism (adult and family/infant) we thank God in confident anticipation and pray to him on the basis of his sure promise of grace.

Why is the faith-response vital? Not to achieve salvation (only God does that) but to receive it; not to make it, but to show it forth in daily life.

The writer numbers many baptist Christians among his closest family and friends, and has the very highest respect for and gratitude towards them. This present exposition *could* be wrong. The aim is not really to persuade people to change churches. It *is* hoped to show that the case for Christian family baptism is sincerely founded on biblical theology alone, and provides a more appropriate way to evangelize and nurture the child of the Christian family.

9
Discrimination in baptism

To clarify biblical theology is one thing, to apply it consistently in practice is another. Differences come to the surface, and tensions are inevitably felt, when Christian teaching comes to be applied in concrete circumstances. At this point the context in which theology is learned, worked out and applied is of considerable (though often underestimated) influence. Moreover there is a psychological and methodological contrast between those who see theology as primary and the cultural context significant but subservient, and those who see the circumstances of the context in society as primary while the biblical theology is significant but subservient. The contrast has been drawn quite sharply, but there is, in fact, an entire spectrum of views between the two poles. Deep feelings of emotion and security (or insecurity) are touched on here with regard to Scripture, tradition, church and nation, and it is not surprising that the regular bursts of correspondence on the subject in both the secular and religious press are marked by considerable heat, even when there is a doubtful amount of light.

The idea of discrimination concerning the candidates for baptism raises deep feelings of bewilderment and resentment — more particularly when the discrimination concerns babies. Babies are lovely and innocent and deserve the best! To set conditions, let alone to refuse baptism to parents, especially to young mothers in the emotional aftermath of pregnancy and first childbirth, is a path that is likely to be fraught with misunderstanding, pain and anguish. The issues need to be considered with care and judgement.

It is worth noticing at the outset, however, that pastoral discrimination is a concept that is acceptable in other areas. Where adults are baptized, confirmed and admitted to Holy Communion they are expected to declare their faith, to receive instruction and share in church life in such a way that the declaration is credible. In ordination there are stringent procedures of discrimination. Everyone would agree that the most careful procedures of discrimination are appropriate in cases of application for '(re-)baptism'. Personal anguish and emotional expectation are significant but are clearly not the only (or even the major) factors in the pastoral situation. In all these pastoral situations judgement will be made (one way or the other) on the basis of a mixture of theological understanding and pastoral insight against a background of the rules and traditions of the Church. All three of these dimensions are open for critical re-examination.

Discrimination in baptism is no longer the preserve of a few idiosyncratic individuals, nor of small reformist pressure groups nor of any particular theological tradition. Clergy and committed lay people alike are increasingly concerned that there should be proper baptism policies, and anxious about indiscriminate baptism. We remind ourselves again that the highly influential World Council of Churches Report *Baptism, Eucharist and Ministry* said that those who practise infant baptism must reconsider certain aspects of their practice and 'must guard themselves against the practice of apparently indiscriminate baptism and take more seriously their responsibility for the nurture of baptized children to mature commitment to Christ'. Again, the Report says 'It is appropriate to explain in the context of the baptismal service the meaning of baptism as it appears from Scripture (i.e.

the participation in Christ's death and resurrection, conversion, pardoning and cleansing, gift of the Spirit, incorporation into the body of Christ and sign of the Kingdom).'[1]

As in all situations of theological debate we must try to hear the best case of the other side, and beware of imputing motives which are insincere or disreputable. Phraseology like 'rigorist' and 'judgemental' on the one hand or 'careless' and 'slap-dash' on the other may well be justified in a particular situation here or there and (if widespread) be a significant feature in theological interpretation, but it is very difficult to evaluate in any objective fashion and can so easily generate heat rather than light, more annoyance than illumination.

The Case for Discrimination

This issue must be carefully developed. No-one objects to the principle of discrimination as such, as has been noted in the contexts of adult baptism, confirmation, holy communion, and ordination disciplines. But what are the arguments for discrimination? They are three-fold:

1. *Theological integrity* — a concern for God and the gospel. The meaning of baptism in the Scriptures must be kept crystal clear. It is not (primarily) a rite of passage, a naming ceremony, an opportunity for thanksgiving after childbirth nor even dedication (of a child) to God and asking for his blessing. It is God's covenant sign of salvation. It signifies sharing in Christ's death and resurrection. It signifies conversion, cleansing, the gift of the Spirit and incorporation into the body of Christ, the Church. It conveys what it signifies not automatically or unconditionally, but in the context of repentance and faith in the gospel of Jesus Christ. The general baptism of chil-

dren whose parents are Muslim, Hindu or atheist by conviction is as utterly incongruous as the baptism of adults with these religious convictions. The same argument applies where parents are agnostic or indifferent. Baptism is into Christ through the Spirit. It is in the name of, by the authority of, and with the significance given by Almighty God, Father, Son and Spirit. There is one baptism, and only one biblical theology of baptism. If baptism sets the visible boundaries of the church, as in biblical theology it does, then there must be some credibility about those boundaries. Otherwise baptism falls into disrepute, and can virtually cease to be *Christian* baptism at all.

2. *Evangelistic and pastoral opportunity* — a concern for people. In the early Church, baptism was always in the context of gospel preaching and the response, 'What shall we do?' The answer is, 'Be baptized in the context of repentance and trust in Jesus Christ'. Baptism clarifies conversion whether it follows or precedes conscious understanding of it. It does not insist on a stereotype of conversion experience, but does point to the necessity of convertedness, of being turned to Christ, and changed to newness of life. The manifold imagery of baptism is a supreme opportunity for evangelistic proclamation and challenge and pastoral teaching and nurture. The increasing number of adult baptisms of those who have grown up in homes of other religious faiths or of no religious faith at all is a significant feature of the evangelistic and pastoral scene.

3. *Pastoral consistency* — a concern for church and mission. There is an important concern that the mission, message and disciplines of the church will be coherent and consistent. The preaching of the gospel, the encouragement to conversion, the assurance of forgiveness and the administration of the sacraments should be all of a piece. The declarations made by

candidates for baptism, and by parents and sponsors of infants are identical to those of the Service of Confirmation and speak clearly of repentance, conversion and faith. It would plainly be unsatisfactory if adults when baptized did not become communicant members of their church. It is similarly unsatisfactory if parents and godparents of baptized children have no concern to practice their faith in public worship. The mission, message and sacraments are seen to be at odds with each other. The clergy know it and lose their nerve, and the laity know it and are perplexed and confused.

The case against pastoral discrimination in the baptism of adults has not been made (at least not since the cessation of the use of *force* in conversion), but the arguments for general or non-discriminating baptism of infants are still sometimes advanced, though with an increasing diffidence. The most recent major written study is *Forbid them not* by R. R. Osborn.[2] He argues that baptism is essentially a sign of God's grace and effective in conveying God's love, forgiveness and life to the recipient. It provides the means and opportunity for the response of faith. England is the supreme example (he argues) of the phenomenon of Christendom, the fusion of church and nation. This means that Englishmen by birth share a repentance for the death of Christ and breathe the atmosphere of godliness. To require explicit or credible profession of faith from parents is a threat to the incoherent but nonetheless real and important substratum of Christian life in the nation. Such, in brief, is a summary of Osborn's thesis. It is a curious mixture of incoherent theology, evangelistic naïvete, idiosyncratic exposition of Church history and sentimental English nationalism. The great attraction of general baptism is its simplicity of preparation — no questions, no conditions. The great drawbacks are that the large numbers inevitably lead to 'private' baptisms, minimal instruction and widespread failure of any effective development of living faith — as Osborn himself accepts. General baptism at its best is seen as a starting point for individual Christian pilgrimage, for pastoral policy, for Christian education and for the influence of a national church upon the national culture. However, the main objections to 'general baptism' are to be found not only in its inherent problems of theological and pastoral incoherence but also in the positive theological and pastoral grounds for discrimination outlined earlier.

The Developing Pastoral Practice

This has been an area of controversy and confusion through much of this century. The central authorities of the Church of England i.e. the Bishops and General Synod have on several occasions in recent decades debated the subject or closely related issues, but both the liturgical provisions and the Canon Law are interpreted in widely differing ways when it comes to pastoral practice. There have been strong protests down the years against unconditional and indiscriminate baptizing, notably in 1896 by Hensley Henson (later Bishop of Durham), and in 1907 by Roland Allen who resigned his appointment as vicar of Chalfont St. Peter. However, until the middle of the twentieth century the protests made little headway against the general image of the Church of England's gentle but vague liberal catholicism, pragmatic 'best boat to fish from' concept of evangelism, and a largely untheological and anti-sacramental evangelicalism. The Mason-Dix-Thornton school of Anglo-Catholics downgraded baptism by asserting that the gift of the Holy Spirit is (primarily) given in Confirmation. Evangelicals were often embarrassed by infant baptism and regarded conversion and Confirmation as much more significant.

The fresh thinking on baptism in recent decades has emphasized the necessity of faith, and a more complete theology of baptism as the single and complete sacramental rite of Christian initiation. Those developments are sheer gain. However, recent thinking has also been confused on at least two counts. As we have already seen, the defence of infant baptism has often been on the basis of highly debatable evidence from early church history or a reliance on biblical texts which cannot alone bear the weight, instead of a coherent understanding of biblical theology and of God's covenant plan and promise. This has, in turn, led to a widespread acceptance of the maxim that 'adult baptism is the norm'. This is one of those jumbo-statements that includes much truth but into which can be smuggled possibilities of confusion and error. True, there is one baptism and one New Testament theology of baptism. True, adult baptism is the primary feature of a missionary situation, although right from the beginning the reference to 'households' was emphatic historically, and the legitimacy and propriety of the baptism of Christian infants was strong theologically. True, also then, that in the Christian family adult baptism will be exceptional and infant baptism the norm. To give any impression of an uncertain theology of, or second-class character to, infant baptism in a Christian family is to invite even further misunderstandings about the nature of conversion and Christian nurture and exacerbate the divisiveness over 're-baptism'.

Before examining suggestions for pastoral procedures which cohere with the biblical theology we do need to have a careful and sympathetic understanding of the context. This context includes the historical background we inherit in England, and the contemporary situation we face now.

1. *The historical background.* England inherited the concept of Christendom — a christened kingdom. Following the conversion of the Roman Emperor Constantine in the early fourth century, Christianity became the official religion of the Empire. This rapidly led to universal infant baptism in the 'Christian nations'. This social movement was reinforced by the theological teaching of St. Augustine of Hippo (354–430) who taught that children who die unbaptized are in some sense 'lost' and, of course, the infant mortality rate was high.

The leaders of the Protestant Reformation in England (as in other European countries) thus assumed the nation was Christian. It had a Christian inheritance from the Middle Ages, and a Christian monarch who was 'Head' of the Church, and Christian law through Parliament. The Prayer Books and Acts of Uniformity were designed to keep the whole nation together in the way of Christ. The 1552 private service of baptism says: 'The pastors and curates shall oft admonish the people that they defer not the baptism of infants any longer than the Sunday, or other holy day next after the child be born'. The Prayer Book funeral service and burial in consecrated ground was only for the baptized, so the pressure was almost total. These historical facts underlie some of the folk-religious (or even superstitious) dimensions of life still to be found in parts of England today — perhaps particularly in some rural areas and in some of the northern cities.

2. *The growing convictions* about the possibility of discriminating procedures in infant baptism are largely due to new features in the life of both nation and church. Some of these have been described already in chapter 1 (p. 5ff) and so only the headings will be noted again: the western world is increasingly seen to be a largely secularized mission-

field needing evangelism rather than part of a Christendom needing pastoral care; the growing influence of biblical theology leads to a decisive shift from a pragmatic (or merely 'traditional') to a principled viewpoint; there is ever-mounting pressure for agreed policies within co-operative and ecumenically shared ministry; teaching about and experience of a 'baptism of the Holy Spirit' is widespread and must be integrated into the theology and practice of initiation; and, finally, the issue of 're-baptism' throws the issues of merely nominal Christianity and indiscriminate baptism into sharper focus. The involvement of lay people in Church leadership, evangelism and baptismal preparation, and the ecumenical dimensions have prompted many clergy to a radical reappraisal of their pastoral practice.

3. *The pastoral procedures* can take many and varied forms. There are an ever-decreasing number of parishes where the parents simply complete an application form, arrive on a Sunday afternoon for a very brief service with none of the usual congregation present, and are never seen again. That always was scandalous and indefensible. There should always be at the very least, pastoral contact before, teaching during, and systematic attempts at Christian nurture following, the baptism.

Moreover, it is not possible to obey the Church of England's Canon Law without undertaking responsible pastoral procedures which contain an important and necessary element of discrimination. This Canon Law has been thoroughly revised by the General Synod in recent years and thus expresses the present discipline and rules of the Church. However, it is not widely known by the clergy, scarcely known at all by lay people and inconsistently applied by the Bishops.

The relevant Canons are here set out in full:[3]

B 21 Of Holy Baptism

It is desirable that every minister having a cure of souls shall normally administer the sacrament of Holy Baptism on Sundays at public worship when the most number of people come together, that the congregation there present may witness the receiving of them that be newly baptized into Christ's Church, and be put in remembrance of their own profession made to God in their baptism

B 22 Of the Baptism of Infants

1. Due notice, normally of at least a week, shall be given before a child is brought to the church to be baptized.
2. If the minister shall refuse or unduly delay to baptize any such infant, the parents or guardians may apply to the bishop of the diocese, who shall, after consultation with the minister, give such directions as he thinks fit.
3. The minister shall instruct the parents or guardians of an infant to be admitted to Holy Baptism that the same responsibilities rest on them as are in the service of Holy Baptism required of the godparents.
4. No minister shall refuse or, save for the purpose of preparing or instructing the parents or guardians or godparents, delay to baptize any infant within his cure that is brought to the church to be baptized, provided that the due notice has been given and the provisions relating to godparents in these Canons are observed.
5. A minister who intends to baptize any infant whose parents are residing outside the boundaries of his cure, unless the names of such persons or of one of them be on the church electoral roll of the same, shall not proceed to the baptism without having sought the good will of the minister of the parish in which such parents reside.
6. No minister being informed of the weakness or

danger of death of any infant within his cure and therefore desired to go to baptize the same shall either refuse or delay to do so.

7. A minister so baptizing a child in a hospital or nursing home, the parents of the child not being resident in his cure, nor their names on the church electoral roll of the same, shall send their names and address to the minister of the parish in which they reside.

8. If any infant which is privately baptized do afterwards live, it shall be brought to the church and there, by the minister, received into the congregation of Christ's flock according to the form and manner prescribed in and by the office for Private Baptism authorized by Canon B 1.

9. The minister of every parish shall warn the people that without grave cause and necessity they should not have their children baptized privately in their houses.

B 23 Of Godparents and Sponsors

1. For every child to be baptized there shall be not fewer than three godparents, of whom at least two shall be of the same sex as the child and of whom at least one shall be of the opposite sex; save that, when three cannot conveniently be had, one godfather and godmother shall suffice. Parents may be godparents for their own children provided that the child have at least one other godparent.

2. The godparents shall be persons who will faithfully fulfil their responsibilities both by their care for the children committed to their charge and by the example of their own godly living.

3. When one who is of riper years is to be baptized he shall choose three, or at least two, to be his sponsors, who shall be ready to present him at the font and afterwards put him in mind of his Christian profession and duties.

4. No person shall be admitted to be a sponsor or godparent who has not been baptized and confirmed. Nevertheless the minister shall have power to dispense with the requirement of confirmation in any case in which in his judgement need so requires.

B 24 Of the Baptism of such as are of riper years

1. When any such person as is of riper years and able to answer for himself is to be baptized, the minister shall instruct such person, or cause him to be instructed, in the principles of the Christian religion, and exhort him so to prepare himself with prayers and fasting that he may receive this holy sacrament with repentance and faith.
2. At least a week before any such baptism is to take place, the minister shall give notice thereof to the bishop of the diocese or whomsoever he shall appoint for the purpose.
3. Every person thus baptized shall be confirmed by the bishop so soon after his baptism as conveniently may be; that so he may be admitted to the Holy Communion.

B 25 Of the sign of the cross in baptism

The Church of England has ever held and taught, and holds and teaches still, that the sign of the Cross used in baptism is no part of the substance of the sacrament: but, for the remembrance of the Cross, which is very precious to those that rightly believe in Jesus Christ, has retained the sign of it in baptism, following therein the primitive and apostolic Churches.

B 26 Of teaching the young

1. Every minister shall take care that the children and young people within his cure are instructed in the doctrine, sacraments, and discipline of Christ, as the Lord has commanded and as they are set forth in the holy Scriptures, in the Book of Common Prayer, and

especially in the Church Catechism; and to this end he, or some godly and competent persons appointed by him, shall on Sundays or if need be at other convenient times diligently instruct and teach them in the same.

2. All parents and guardians shall take care that their children receive such instruction.

All pastoral practice should be 'pastoral' i.e. shepherd-like, gentle and caring. Practice of discrimination in any area of church life should never be harsh or unloving, and it is tragic if that impression is ever given. There are situations, however, where an element of pastoral judgement by Christian leaders cannot be avoided. This cannot be forbidden by our Lord's warning 'Do not judge, or you too will be judged' (Matthew 7.1). This command is closely followed by two others which require the exercise of critical discernment and discrimination — 'Do not give dogs what is sacred; do not throw your pearls to pigs' (v.6) and 'Watch out for false prophets' (v.15) The attitude Jesus forbids is harsh censoriousness which is destructive and condemning. There are many parents willing to testify 'We are so glad the vicar made us stop and think about the meaning of baptism. It has changed our lives!'

The Canon Law lays down four practical disciplines:

First, ministers are to respect one another's baptism practices. This is achieved by the important stipulation (Canon B 22.5) that a minister, if requested to baptize a child from another parish, will seek the goodwill of the minister of that parish. In this way the undermining of a carefully constructed parish baptism practice is avoided. Of course 'to seek goodwill' for a Christian minister means far more than a cursory letter of information. No Christian minister will baptize against the wish of the parish minister except after very careful thought and (it is suggested) consultation not only with the parish minister involved but also with the bishop.

It is vitally important that bishops support those clergy who are seeking to fulfil these principles, and prevent other clergy from baptizing children indiscriminately from neighbouring parishes.

Secondly, baptism should normally be at a main Sunday service (B 21). This enables the new members to be welcomed properly into the Christian family, and for the whole congregation to be reminded of the sacrament and its rich significance for them all. Practical problems should not be allowed to lead to a regular ignoring of this Canon which has such clear and obvious theological justification. Rather, any practical problems should lead to a critical reconsideration of the parochial practice of worship, initiation, evangelism and nurture of young people in the Christian faith.

Thirdly, godparents or sponsors should be baptized, confirmed (and thus communicant) Christians. This is strongly asserted in B 23.4 and the permitted power to dispense with the requirement should be used sparingly. The permission to use discretion would be of value when suitable godparents are members of another denomination which does not practise confirmation e.g. Baptist, Pentecostal or Brethren. The crucial role of godparents is detailed in B 23.2 and includes 'the example of their own godly living'. Discipline is needed to restore the spiritual character of this custom.

Fourthly, parents and guardians need to receive adequate instruction. It is not good enough briefly to describe the mechanics of the service and give them a leaflet or letter about the meaning of baptism. B 22.3 says unequivocally that the 'same responsibilities' rest on parents as on godparents. This clearly implies baptism, confirmation and 'the example of godly living' (B 23.2,4). B 26 requires parents to ensure continued Christian instruction. The Baptism of Children service in the Alternative Service Book starts with the minister saying:

> Children who are too young to profess the Christian faith are baptized on the understanding that they are brought up as Christians within the family of the Church. As they grow up, they need the help and encouragement of that family, so that they learn to be faithful in public worship and private prayer, to live by trust in God, and come to confirmation.
> Parents and godparents, the *children* whom you have brought for baptism *depend* chiefly on you for the help and encouragement *they need*. Are you willing to give it to *them* by your prayers, by your example, and by your teaching?

to which the parents and godparents reply 'I am willing'.

There is no ambiguity later in the part of the service called 'The Decision'. The minister says:

> Those who bring children to be baptized must affirm their allegiance to Christ and their rejection of all that is evil.
> It is your duty to bring up *these children* to fight against evil and to follow Christ.
>
> Therefore I ask these questions which you must answer for yourselves and for *these children*.
> Do you turn to Christ?
> *Answer*: I turn to Christ
> Do you repent of your sins?
> *Answer*: I repent of my sins
> Do you renounce evil?

Answer: I renounce evil.

and later

You have brought *these children* to baptism. You must now declare before God and his Church the Christian faith into which *they are* to be baptized, and in which you will help *them* to grow. You must answer for yourselves and for *these children*.
Do you believe and trust in God the Father who made the world?
Answer: I believe and trust in him.
Do you believe and trust in his Son Jesus Christ, who redeemed mankind?
Answer: I believe and trust in him.
Do you believe and trust in his Holy Spirit, who gives life to the people of God?
Answer: I believe and trust in him.

It is therefore clear that both the law and the liturgy of the Church of England require parents bringing a child to be baptized to be confessing, practising Christians themselves. In 1974 the General Synod reiterated 'the view that Infant Baptism should continue to be available to the children of all parents that request it and are willing *and able* to make the requisite promises'.

The Service of Thanksgiving for the Birth of a Child is available in the Alternative Service Book, page 213. This involves acknowledgement of God's gift and love, and prayer for his blessing, but is neither based on confessed Christian commitment nor implies the fullness of the covenant relationship of blessing and obligation. It can be used as an element of teaching–evangelism hopefully leading into family-conversion, covenant-commitment and household-baptism.

It is frequently a cause of public controversy when

a clergyman requires the parents to attend church worship before the baptism of their baby. Such a requirement can be justified on many grounds. To participate in Christian worship and congregational life is clearly a most important part of instruction in Christian life. All good instruction should be experienced where possible and not just cerebral. Baptism is 'into Christ' and into 'the body of Christ' the Church. It is a nonsense to divorce it from the congregational life. If the parents are promising a 'godly example' there must be some credibility to their profession and promise. Worship, holy communion and church membership are not optional aspects of Christian life, parenthood and nurture. The Church does grave disservice to God and his gospel to leave any grounds for people thinking they are.

When parents who are not communicant church members apply for the baptism of a child, there should be a clear parish-wide pastoral strategy. This begins with warm congratulations, a visit, and information about the 'mothers and babies group' and crèche facilities during morning worship. Then it must be explained that the church is delighted to offer a service of Thanksgiving and prayer either in the home or the church. Baptism, however, implies a definite Christian faith, and commitment to Christ and the Church. There is a preparation course of 4–6 weeks which might include Sunday worship. Many parishes use *Good News down the street* by M. Wooderson[4] or a pattern similar to P. Ball in *Journey into Faith'*.[5] It is of the greatest value if lay people play a major role in this preparation. The style and content will vary according to the culture and area, but it should involve a major investment of thought and effort. This is front-line evangelism and pastoral care. Its aim is to bring parents to faith, or to clearer faith in Christ, and understanding of Christian life.

Unfortunately, the Faith and Order Advisory

Group of the Church of England has made a most ambivalent and unsatisfactory response to *Baptism, Eucharist and Ministry*[6] on this particular issue. They admit the offence where baptism is granted in a situation where those applying 'do not seem to have given any evidence of wanting to be identified with Jesus Christ and his Church'. On the other hand, they warn against 'over-discriminating' and requiring 'unreasonable evidence of the authenticity of their faith' (para. 45). We expect more than a re-statement of the problem from FOAG. We expect theological guidelines for pastoral practice. Their subsequent assertion 'So called "indiscriminate baptism" reflects a view of the Church as a "mixed community"; a more rigorous policy emphasizes the "gathered" nature of the Church' is unhelpfully superficial. The visible Church will always to some extent be both 'mixed' and 'gathered'. The more searching questions are about the significance of baptism, and whether the Church has any credible boundaries at all. It is paradoxical that in para. 121 they say, 'Only an explicit common understanding of the nature of the Church and its role as a *credible and effective sign*, instrument and sacrament of salvation will provide a secure foundation for the reconciliation of churches' (my italics), but then later say 'There is evidence that in the Church of England most of those baptized never become communicants and it is highly probable that their personal religion is not of the "converted" kind described in the Lima Text'. Questions are asked about 'apparently indiscriminate baptism' including issues of nurture and education and 'Do questions relating to faith, the key to commitment in the Church, feature enough in our Synods?' They give no answer. My answer is that Bishops, Synods, FOAG and the entire Church must be more clear, consistent and credible in their biblical theology and pastoral practice. Actions speak louder than words.

The policy of general baptism has had a long innings but has clearly not stemmed the rising tide of secularism and unbelief. Both theological integrity and the radically-changed social situation call for a loving but firm discipline of discrimination in the administration of the Lord's sacrament and covenant-sign.

10

'Re-baptism' — Is it ever justified?

The New Testament writers affirm that there is *one* baptism (Ephesians 4.5) into the one Lord Jesus Christ. There is one biblical theology of baptism, although the various Christian churches may not equally or fully embrace and teach that theology. A second baptism is, in the strict sense of the term, non-sense — it is a self-contradiction. Either the first so-called 'baptism' was really not a baptism and so the second one was a baptism, or the first one was baptism and the second one was not. But there cannot be *two* baptismal initiations into the Christian life. How has any suggestion or debate about 're-baptism' come about?

The request for 're-baptism'

The issue is increasingly common in recent years although it has been known for centuries. It is more complex than is often realized, and so the issues will be illustrated by some typical cases.[1]

1. *The Adult convert* George is 25 and religion has held no meaning in his life. Now suddenly he has come to know Jesus Christ in a vivid, personal, life-transforming way. He is eager to join the church. As he reads the Acts of the Apostles he sees baptism as the way to express his new relationship with God and his people. However, when he discusses it with his vicar it transpires that he was baptized as a baby, and so the vicar kindly but firmly indicates that another baptism is quite out of the question. George is perplexed because his parents never attended

church and did not bring him up in the Lord or in the church. What could that splashing with water on the little baby mean? and what has it got to do with the excitement and reality of his new-found life in Christ?

A similar problem confronted Sheila who is in her thirties. She went to a Youth Club in a church where they practised 'believer baptism'. At the age of twelve she went to a Christian holiday houseparty and the leaders pressed the young people to follow Jesus. Several of her friends asked to be baptized and Sheila did not want to be out of step with the gang of friends. She said the right things, was baptized, but a year or two later she stopped going to church. Now twenty years later she knows that she has met with Jesus in a real way and wishes to commit her life to him and the Church. As she looks back on her childhood she is grateful for Christian youth leaders but doubtful of the wisdom of their pressurizing children into 'decision' and almost completely sure that her profession of faith and baptism was due to external pressures. How should she, now, proclaim her mature discipleship and desire to join the Church?

2. *Moving to a 'baptist' church.* Mary's parents are deeply committed Christians. Mary was baptized as a baby and grew up from her earliest days to know God and love Jesus Christ. She gladly went to church with the family, and although there were ups and downs in her faith and discipleship, she never regretted being confirmed at the age of 14. Mary has married a Christian man who has moved around many parts of the country and attended many churches of different denominations. On moving to a new area they find themselves close to a lively Baptist church where their children have good friends. They want to be full members, but the church requires that Mary be baptized. What is she to do? Does she

effectively renounce her infant baptism that has meant so much to her as God's covenant-sign, and her parents' godly unbringing? Or does she threaten the family unity and full involvement in their local church?

3. *'Charismatic' renewal.* Fred grew up in a Christian home, was baptized and confirmed and has always been glad to be a member of the church. It was important to him, but if truth be told, it was not exciting. In his mid-twenties he went to a charismatic conference and had a deep experience of spiritual renewal and reality. His awareness of the personal intimacy of God as Abba, father, brought him to a radically new joy in worship, prayer and reading the Bible. He felt as though he could tell everyone about Jesus, and remarkable signs of God's power resulted from his prayers, witness and gifts. 'If this is "baptism in the Spirit"', he reasoned, 'should it not be testified to or expressed in "baptism in water"?' The vicar is delighted that Fred has 'come alive' in his faith but cannot even consider a second baptism. Fred just wants to demonstrate somehow the overwhelming change that has made such an impact on his life.

In real life, George may find a Baptist Church or Brethren Assembly where he can be baptized, and perhaps, return to his Church of England parish with mixed feelings of perplexity, sadness and embarrassment. Sheila would almost certainly not be offered a 're-baptism' in a Baptist Church. She might be tempted into a 'House-church' where the theology of baptism is less significant than its experience, but either way is not a happy solution for her. Mary might decide to go through 'believer baptism' in order to join the church with her husband, but is sad to hurt her parents and does not see the ceremony as baptism into Christ, but just a rite of entry to that particular church. Fred will either get stuck in to his local church in a more committed way or go off to a 'house-church' of similar-minded folk. But will his decision be based on scriptural and theological considerations or on his own subjective feelings and emotional needs?

The charismatic movement has, in some situations, reinforced the sacramental dimension of the outward expression of the reality of God's grace. In other contexts it leads to a down-grading of the significance of sacramental signs compared with the experienced reality of 'baptism in Spirit'. The individuals in the stories and the Christian leaders they consult should think not only in terms of 'what is right for them?' but also 'what is right?' The emphasis in much pastoral work is 'non-directive' or person-centred rather than truth-centred. This can reinforce a personalized and subjective view of Christian faith, church and sacraments which loses touch with the given-ness of God's word in Scripture and the necessity for order and discipline in church life.

The case against 're-baptism'

The question 'What is right?' implies theological judgement rather than a reliance on merely subjective feeling. The depth of emotional need (or even anguish) is not the only, or even the most significant factor. It *is* significant but other kinds of response may be possible. There are formidable arguments against 're-baptism'.

1. *Theologically*, the very nature and meaning of baptism is at stake. There is *one* baptism, says Paul the apostle. There are not separate baptisms for different churches, nor to represent different experiences. Baptism must be seen (like holy communion)

as primarily a sign God gives us rather than a symbol we undergo for him. It is God's covenant-sign which must be met by faith. The relationship in time between the baptism and the faith may not always be tidy or certain, but the sign is not made invalid by untidiness or uncertainties about quality of faith. Validity and efficacy must be distinguished. Validity must depend on objective factors, even though efficacy is a matter known only to God. (See the discussion on p. 89). the major argument against 're-baptism' is a proper understanding of the meaning of baptism in itself (see pp. 17–30). Chapter 6 needs to be thoroughly digested, as also Chapters 7 and 8.

If baptism (of infant or adult) does not appear to have been a credible initiation into Christ and his Church, then there is a theological anomaly and pastoral problem. However, any repetition of baptism might meet the emotional needs of some individuals, but at the expense of further theological confusion for all and pastoral problems in the future.

2. *Pastorally*, the dependence of the reality or validity of a baptism on any kind of subjective consideration means that some people might never be certain about their baptism and repeatedly seek to renew it. New Testament theology encourages Christians to be confident about God's covenant love and the security of their salvation in Christ but every Church leader knows Christians who are either occasionally or even regularly subjected to bouts of insecurity and lack of assurance. It would surely be a pastoral (and theological) tragedy if the move to different churches was marked by another 'baptism'.

The World Council of Churches report *Baptism, Eucharist and Ministry*[2] says unambiguously 'Baptism is an unrepeatable act. Any practice which might be interpreted as "re-baptism" must be avoided.'

The *Church of England* and Roman Catholic Church baptize believing adults and infant children of parents who confess their faith. This is followed by confirmation when the candidate is old enough to assume personal responsibility. Christian baptism of other churches is recognized and cannot be repeated, although there is a form of 'conditional' baptism where there is genuine uncertainty about whether a person has been baptized or not (see ASB p. 279). Discrimination about baptism varies widely. Some Anglicans (including clergy) are uneasy about infant baptism altogether and use a service of thanksgiving or infant dedication followed by 'believer' baptism later in life.

The *Methodist* Church has broadly similar practice and diversity. The Methodist Conference has ruled against re-baptism but has stressed the need for more opportunity for public testimony as a means of giving expression to deeper spiritual experience. Some use a re-dedication service involving immersion in water and making clear it is not baptism, but this is not authorized.

The *Baptist* Union churches do not agree on the necessity for 'believers' baptism' (or any baptism) as a condition for church membership. Some would say that Mary (in the story on p. 151) need not, and probably should not, be '(re)-baptized'. Thus some would recognize the validity of an infant baptism involving believing parents followed by profession of conscious faith in confirmation. On the other hand, many (probably most) Baptist pastors would baptize George (p. 150) on the grounds that the circumstances of his 'baptism' rendered it meaningless. However, it would be very rare (perhaps impossible) to find a pastor to 're-baptize' Sheila in spite of their emphasis on baptism following and expressing faith. Finally, many would 'baptize' Mary if she requested it with strong personal conviction.

The official Baptist Union response to *BEM*[3] objects strongly to indiscriminate baptism rather than to infant baptism itself. They say the section on 're-baptism' (quoted above) is 'wholly unacceptable in its present form' . . . 'In cases of infant baptism which are neither accompanied nor followed by any of the significant features of the initiatory process to which the Report amply draws attention and where the individual involved is convinced out of an instructed conscience that Christian obedience requires believer baptism, we cannot agree that an *a priori* universal bar should operate'.

There is a strong element of individual decision and local variation in Baptist Churches. When one moves beyond the Baptist Union to independent chapels, Brethren Assemblies and 'house-churches' it becomes almost impossible to generalize on their baptismal practices in these situations.

The *United Reformed* Church accommodates both infant and believer baptism while formally declaring re-baptism unacceptable. The Churches of Christ (following Baptist practice) have recently merged with the URC. Both modes are to continue and 'nothing should be done in conformity with one practice that casts doubt on the integrity of the other'. No minister is required to perform a mode of baptism to which he has conscientious objection. Most of the united churches in the URC follow their traditional pattern of initiation.

This dual system is in operation in several areas of ecumenical experiment. It is any request for 're-baptism' which threatens a delicate situation. In the United Church of North India, the local bishop decides the policy at this most sensitive point.

Pastoral care and provision

Considerable gentleness, pastoral and teaching skills are needed to cope with requests for 're-baptism' particularly when the applications are in the context of strong emotional experience and/or peer pressure. There are many parallels with the pastoral problems of discrimination in applications for 'first' baptism. Three dimensions of pastoral care and provision are needed:

1. *To reduce the scale of the problem* it is important, where possible, to take certain steps before the issue arises. In fact the problem can be largely pre-empted in this way:

(a) regular and careful *teaching* about the significance of baptism including the nature of God's covenant love, plan and signs and the place of the sacraments in God's provision for church life. It is only *good* teaching that will keep out bad teaching. Too often there has been a vacuum on this subject which has inevitably been filled by subjective and erroneous ideas. This will be given more attention in chapter 11.

(b) *careful discrimination* over initial candidature for baptism of both adult and infant will significantly reduce both the size and the bitterness of the problem. It is the feeling of hurt and loss through the abuse of baptism in the case-study of George (p. 150) that is so difficult to deal with. Indiscriminate baptism devalues the sacrament and provides substantial theological, pastoral and emotional grounds for George's dilemma. The *BEM* Report says about this issue: 'This contributes to the reluctance of churches which practise believers' baptism to acknowledge the validity of infant baptism; this fact should lead to more critical reflection on the meaning of baptism, within those majority churches themselves' (i.e. in Europe and North America).[4] It is quite clear from the Baptist Union response and the writings of other Baptist theologians that for many of them the *real* scandal and stumbling-block is at this point of indiscriminate use of baptism rather than the baptism of children of believing parents. The Church of England response[5] does not show a clear enough appreciation of this crucial dimension of the problem.

(c) good relationships and *consultation* between church leaders in a locality will increasingly mean that baptism is seen not as a matter for individual whim or even the concern of a single church, but a joy for the whole Church of God in Christ Jesus. So 're-baptism' is a concern not just for the individual and a local church but for the whole Church. It is hoped that leaders would consult and pray together even where they finally cannot agree. It is at this point that questions of initiation are especially difficult with Christian groups that have no clear leadership, or are recently schismatic or who regard other denominations as heretical or beyond fellowship. In parts of the country 'House-church' or 'Restorationist' leaders are realizing the value of better relationships, co-operation and consultation but time is needed for the healing of some wounds of division.

2. *To offer a significant alternative* to the 'adult convert' and to the 'spiritually renewed'. The person most in need of pastoral provision of a public and liturgical character is George the adult convert whose infant baptism was apparently in the context of parental unbelief and led to no nurture in Christ. He needs assurance that he can still look back to that baptism as God's sign of his covenant-love, but he also needs a suitably joyful and impressive ceremony in which he can both testify to his new-found faith and 'be confirmed' by the prayer, the welcome, and the joy of the Christian community. The provision may be the service of Confirmation itself. It may be in the context of a regular congregational Renewal of Baptismal Vows (*ASB* p. 276). The Methodist annual Covenant renewal service (often used at the first

Sunday of the new year) is increasingly used in other churches. Services of Marriage renewal are becoming popular, and many dioceses offer an annual opportunity for clergy to renew their ordination vows. Some element of testimony or spoken response is important, and some element of dramatic action which meets the emotional need for expression of renewal.

The idea of renewing baptismal vows in or with water is being canvassed. (The Doctrine Commission of the Presbyterian Church of New Zealand's provision was authorized by their General Assembly, November 1977.)[6] This meets the pressure for a rite symbolizing washing or an immersion symbolizing death and resurrection with Christ. First there is an introductory address emphasizing the significance of the earlier baptism as God's gift and action, and the subsequent acceptance by the candidate of God's grace through the Spirit in repentance and faith. Then after affirmation of faith the minister immerses the candidate saying appropriate words such as:

'As you were baptized in the name of the Father and of the Son and of the Holy Spirit, so now I confirm to you the cleansing, forgiveness, new life and promised gift of God's Spirit which are in his covenant'

or

'As into Jesus Christ you were baptized, so I pray God who began a good work in you, to bring it to completion at the day of Christ Jesus'.

The grave theological and pastoral problem associated with this 'sacramental and liturgical brinkmanship'[7] is that what people *hear* is as significant as what the minister has to *say*. Although the minister will say it is not baptism, the congregation (and the candidate) will all too easily hear and see it as such, and the validity of all baptisms will be undermined. On the other hand indiscriminate baptism using the

New Testament language of efficacy where there is no credible profession of faith is also 'liturgical and sacramental brinkmanship'. It would be better to do without either but until we get rid of the latter, the pressure for the former could become overwhelming. Should the church lose some of its best members over this issue?

3. *To accept some untidiness* is probably necessary in an imperfect world and in imperfect church life. Bishop Colin Buchanan has argued that not only should Christians be dissuaded from 're-baptism' but also, if they have received it, they should be urged to repent, to renounce it and sign a certificate of renunciation[8] e.g. 'I . . ., having received Christian baptism at . . . on . . . was subsequently 're-baptized' at . . . on . . . I now renounce any belief that this 're-baptism' was in fact my Christian baptism, and I revert to my original baptism as my true Christian baptism. Signed: . . .

This is quite logical in terms of theology, and is probably important for ordination candidates. They must work through this sacramental issue before they have responsibility for theological and pastoral leadership to others. However, there are considerable pastoral problems in pursuing the policy of renunciation further. What sanctions would be appropriate, if any? At what point, and for how long, should pressure be applied? It is arguable that some untidiness can be permitted even if with a heavy heart. The earlier proposals to reduce the scale of the problem are the most significant contributions to this issue.

11

Living and preaching baptism

Baptism is a ceremony, but a ceremony that provides a pattern and shape for the whole of Christian life. It is not so much a single service or event, more a way of life. The truth of baptism as an event will only be understood when the reality of baptism as a way of life is lived and experienced.

The World Council of Churches Faith and Order Commission Paper[1] speaks of the high significance of baptism for the practical life of the Church. It says:

> since baptism encompasses the whole Christian life, lack of clarity concerning the meaning of baptism leads to uncertainty all along the line. It is beyond dispute that in no church body does baptism have the decisive significance which the witness of the New Testament ascribes to it. Here we all have much to learn. A serious penetration into the meaning of baptism and an appropriation of the treasure given in baptism would give *preaching* and *teaching* both a centrally focussed content and a new breadth, together with an insight which clarifies and unifies the whole of christian life. The more the baptized learn to see their whole life in the light of their baptism, the more does their life take on the pattern of life 'in Christ'.

Living Baptism

The baptism event provides a pattern and shape for the baptized life. The baptized life is the life of Christ, life in and through Christ, Christian life, a converted life. Just as the marriage ceremony is a decisive event but must then be worked out through married life, so too baptism is a decisive event but must be worked out through Christian life. Just as the marriage ceremony marks the beginning of a new way of life, so too with baptism. Baptism is for living.

1. *Baptism enshrines encouragement* and unequivocally focusses the life of dicipleship of Jesus Christ. The divine blessings symbolized in and offered through baptism are entirely offered in and through Jesus Christ. The gift of baptism understood as covenant sign reminds the believer of the priority and initiative of God's grace, of the faithfulness of God's covenant promise through the ages, and of the incredible costliness of God's salvation in Christ. As in the other sacrament ordained by Christ, the Lord's Supper, there is no greater encouragement than to be turned back to Christ as the centre, the focus and the determining factor of life. The blessings of baptism have been spelled out on p. 76. Christian people need constantly reminding that in baptism they are forgiven and cleansed, they belong to and are identified with Jesus, they share in the significance of his death and resurrection, they receive the gift of the Holy Spirit, they are adopted as children of God and become members of the Body of Christ, the Church. We have seen that these blessings are not automatic or unconditional but are offered through the gospel to those who receive that good news by faith. Here is great encouragement for the believer. Here is the basis for a pastor saying to the troubled Christian 'You are baptized'. On the other hand . . .

2. *Baptism clarifies commitment* for its blessings in Christ clearly imply discipleship to Christ. The blessings *from* him will not be enjoyed unless there is continuing faith *in* him and submission *to* him. The

baptized life is a Christ-centred and Christ-empowered life — apart from him we can do nothing.

The multiple significance of baptism gives a definite shape to the Christian's commitment. Having been cleansed and forgiven, there must be a continuing concern for holiness and purity of life. Having been identified with Jesus Christ, there must be a continuing submission to him, and life through him. Having participated in his death and resurrection, there must be a continuing putting to death the deeds of the sinful nature and a continuing setting of the mind on resurrection life. Having been baptized with the Spirit, there must be a continuing walking by the spirit being filled with thc Spirit, showing the fruit of the Spirit and using properly gifts of the Spirit. Having been born again into God's family, there must be a continuing life of acknowledging God as Abba, Father, and developing the family likeness. Having been baptized into the body of Christ, the Church, there must be a continuing life of Christian fellowship, inter-dependence and service. thus baptism expresses the dimensions of all that God offers, and, at the same time, clarifies the nature of the appropriate response.

It cannot be over-emphasized that God's blessings are neither automatic nor unconditional. Thus baptism must only be understood, offered and received in the context of the gospel of Jesus, received by faith and issuing in a life of discipleship. Christian life is a baptism-shaped life, and Christian ethics are 'baptism ethics'. When Paul was speaking of the necessity of holiness he repeatedly reminded his hearers of baptism.

> We died to sin; how can we live in it any longer? Or don't you know that all of us who were baptized into Christ Jesus were baptized into his

> death? We were therefore buried with him through baptism into death in order that, just as Christ was raised from the dead through the glory of the Father, we too may live a new life. (Romans 6.3–4).

That is classic baptism ethics.

When Paul was arguing for the unity of Christians he repeatedly refers to the significance of baptism. Baptism is not 'into the name of Paul' or any human leader but only into Christ. 'We were all baptized by one Spirit into one body.' There is one baptism. (1 Corinthians 12.13).

Baptism is no more mere theoretical theology than it is mere ceremonial rite — it is profoundly practical, and relevant to the individual life of the Christian and corporate life of the Church. Just as there are no blessings in Christ which are not symbolized in baptism, there are no aspects of discipleship and obedience that are not implied by or consequent upon baptism.

Augustine thought of baptism as like a soldier's badge or uniform. It is, he said, the same sign which both identifies the soldier and convicts the deserter. Baptism then enshrines all the encouragement of God's covenant promises but it also reinforces all the responsibilities of God's covenant requirements.

Like a wedding ring, baptism joyfully reminds the Christian of the love and commitment *of* the One who gives it. It also reminds of the obligation of faithfulness *to* that One who 'loved me and gave himself for me'.

Preaching Baptism

'I am convinced', wrote the Scottish theologian D. M. Baillie, 'that the people of the Church need far more teaching than we have been accustomed to give them on the sacraments . . . As regards baptism . . . a great many of our faithful church folk are in a complete fog about its meaning — which is a dreadful condition of affairs.'[2] Pierre Marcel, the French theologian wrote 'If no place is found for preaching, and precisely this (covenant of grace) preaching on which the legitimacy of infant baptism is founded, what can baptism be except a rite deprived of its content and meaning?[3]

The reason for the assertion of the Faith and Order Commission that 'in no church body does baptism have the decisive significance which the witness of the New Testament ascribes to it' is because there is little preaching and teaching about baptism that is fully biblical. So much of the theology is diluted by folk religion on the one hand or 'witness to faith response' on the other. So much of the practice is indiscriminate or private on the one hand or individual and 'personal conscience' on the other. Where the clergy are weak in theology and embarrassed about the practice, it is little wonder that the lay people are 'in a complete fog'. Baptism needs to be preached because:

1. *It provides illustration*. This is a major answer to *why* baptism should be preached. The New Testament writers never provide a systematic study of baptism. They use it again and again to illustrate the deepest significance of life in Christ. It illustrates a great range of the aspects of God's blessings through Christ. It speaks of washing, anointing, sprinkling, dying, burial, rising. It is particularly used to illustrate the decisiveness of new life in Christ and, therefore, the consequent expectation of holiness in personal life, and unity in Church life.

Baptism is primarily a gift given to us and thus illustrates the initiative of God's grace. It points us outside ourselves to the Christ into whom we are baptized, and to the objective events of his life in the power of which, by faith, we now share. The power of the illustration in preaching depends considerably on the power and significance of the experienced event. This is where many a baptism of infants loses out to baptisms of adults. Too often the theology and significance is attenuated and the dramatic sense of occasion minimal. There is inevitably a circular chicken-and-egg argument here. Baptism will not be properly administered until there is clearer theology and preaching, and there will not be clear theology and preaching until there is proper administration. The development, then, must go hand in hand. The Church cannot afford to lose this potent source of illustration.

2. *It needs explanation*. This is part of the answer to *how* baptism should be preached. There has been profound misunderstanding of the nature of covenant signs and the significance of the sacraments when the climate of thought has been religious and even Christian. How much more incomprehension there will be in an increasingly secularist and multi-faith context. The origins, development and fulfilment of God's covenant plan need explanation. This involves a proper understanding of the relation of the two testaments, and of promise and fulfilment. The nature of grace and faith, and the relation of covenant promise, sign and obligation need exposition.

The meaning of sacrament needs explanation with its relation of word and action. Furthermore there is widespread ignorance of the Old Testament among Christians, so many do not appreciate the family principle, or the profoundly spiritual character of grace, faith and obedience in the experience of the saints before Christ. Although this section is short, these explanatory issues which lie behind a proper understanding of baptism will be found throughout the earlier chapters.

Christian congregations increasingly need to understand the foundations of sound theological thinking. An adequate authority will be found not in the early church practice or in odd biblical 'proof' texts, but in a carefully interpreted exposition of the biblical patterns of God's action in salvation. This biblical theology of baptism with its careful and crucial covenant balance of grace and faith, efficacy and conditionality throws light upon the nature of the person of Christ, his atoning work and our experience of salvation.

The tools for understanding baptism are an appreciation of covenant, of sacrament and of the family in biblical teaching. Many preachers fail to teach these 'big' subjects. It is increasingly clear that mini-teaching (by mini-preachers) leads to mini-understanding and so produces mini-Christians.

3. *It involves obligation* for both parents and church leaders. This is the answer to the question *by whom* baptism should be preached. Parents are to bring up their children 'in the training and instruction of the Lord' (Ephesians 6.4). Too many Christian parents have lost their nerve altogether in the areas of training and discipline. However, Christian faith and life needs to be caught as well as taught, and the Christian home is the supreme opportunity for that long-term gradual growth in Christian faith, practice and understanding. The responsibility cannot be passed away to others whether in Church or school.

God's intention for a growth from childhood in understanding his covenant love and covenant life is nowhere more clearly seen than in Deuteronomy 6.

> Hear, O Israel: the Lord our God, the Lord is one. Love the Lord your God with all your heart,

> and with all your soul and with all your strength. These commandments that I give you today are to be upon your hearts. Impress them on your children. Talk about them when you sit at home, and when you walk along the road, when you lie down and when you get up (v. 4–7).

There follows instructions about phylacteries for hand and forehead and the *mezuzah* for doorposts. These little containers with portions of God's word in them remind the Jewish family that every action and thought and every part of daily life is for submission to the Word of the Covenant Lord (v. 8–9). Parents were to be prepared to explain to their children about God's salvation, covenant signs and obligations (v. 20–25). Following Christ's coming, the ideal is for children to grow up like Timothy who 'from infancy had known the holy scriptures, which are able to make you wise for salvation through faith in Christ Jesus' (2 Timothy 3.15).

There is, in addition, a major obligation for church leaders to teach about baptism too. It needs to be taught positively to those who have been baptized i.e. 'You have been baptized into Christ as Saviour and Lord. Now live for him, and in him.' It is true that people cannot with impunity point to their baptisms (whether adult or infant) and then live carelessly and ignore the obligations of covenant life in Christ. It is also true that people should not place confidence in their parenthood or upbringing. Nevertheless, Christian teaching which warns against 'sacramentalism' or 'hereditary godliness' must be careful not to reduce the God-given significance of his covenant-signs and of the family-context. The best way to teach the significance of baptism in the church-context is in the course of the baptism service itself. Here, action and practice will speak louder than words. Roger Lloyd wrote[4] 'Our practice of baptizing every baby presented to us regardless of whether there is the least likelihood or even possibility of its being trained to be a Christian not only makes nonsense of the whole doctrine of the Church as we have received it, but also (and precisely because it does so) it seriously hampers and embarrasses the whole witness and proclamation of the Church'.

The obligation, then, rests on parents and church leaders to explain baptism, and to use it to illustrate Christian living.

Appendix: The baptism of Jesus — and ours

When preaching and teaching about Old Testament covenant signs and even the baptism of John, careful note of both the continuities and discontinuities is important in relation to baptism.

There are specially rich and suggestive parallels between the baptism of Jesus (see Chapter 5) and Christian baptism. These parallels are theologically important and devotionally rich, but nevertheless the baptisms must be clearly distinguished. The baptism of Jesus was quite unique — both as a baptism of John, and in any comparison with later Christian baptism. His baptism as an adult for instance is irrelevant to the controversial issue of an appropriate age for Christian initiation now. The baptism of Jesus was not 'initiation into Christ' and, therefore, straight lines cannot be drawn and implications must be carefully considered. Nevertheless the four issues of major theological significance in the baptism of Jesus have parallels in Christian baptism —

1. Jesus was *identified* with sinners — we are identified with Jesus Christ. We are baptized into him, into his name. God says 'I will identify you with my son, Jesus Christ'.
2. Jesus was committed to *sacrificial death* — we are

baptized into Jesus' death, in order to die to the old life. The baptized are to count themselves dead to sin (Romans 6.11).

3. Jesus was anointed with the *Holy Spirit* — we are baptized in the Spirit into the body of Christ 'the Anointed One'. The Spirit then equips with power for new life and service.

4. Jesus was assured of *sonship*, albeit servant-sonship — we are assured of adoption and cry 'Abba, Father'. We too are heirs with Christ, if we suffer with him (Romans 8.15–17).

12

Forward together?

This book has inevitably dealt with matters of considerable controversy. Like the Report *Baptism, Eucharist and Ministry*, however, its aim is to secure a greater measure of unity where possible, and of mutual understanding where unity is not at present possible. Where serious inadequacy of theology, practice and the understanding of authority underlying these is perceived, argument and debate is part of the Christian responsibility of truth and love. In this final chapter, then, we ask the question whether Christians can move forward together in this area.

It seems clear from the recent literature that Christians might agree on the following aspects of baptism:

(a) It is God's sign of his saving blessings in Christ.
(b) It also symbolizes the necessary response to God of faith.
(c) It is an initiation which should lead to life-long growth into Christ.
(d) It should be celebrated and developed in the Christian community.
(e) It is unrepeatable.

These five assertions are not really controversial although some traditions of Christianity have not given full weight to some of them.

In the light of these areas of agreement, and the giving of due weight to each one of them, can we move forward together in traditional areas of disagreement?

The Mode of Baptism

Anglicans have always acknowledged the propriety of immersion but have not insisted it is necessary or the norm. Perhaps all churches could begin to make proper provision for baptism by immersion as a method of administration as some Anglican churches are now doing. General Synod could recommend methods of implementation. Even where pouring or sprinkling is used it is important to use a substantial amount of water rather than a few drops or even a damp wipe. Baptist writings argue for immersion because of the important symbolism of burial in Romans 6. However, many of their recent writings are much more concerned with the response of living faith, and, where that is apparent at the baptism or later, are willing to accept the validity of baptism administered in forms other than immersion.

Where there is firm commitment to the five aspects of baptism at the beginning of the chapter, it is hoped that the amount of water used at baptism would not prevent Christians moving forward together.

Believers and Infants

The Church of England does not insist on its members baptizing their infants, and it could clarify the availability of two patterns of administration — infant baptism followed by affirmation of faith in Confirmation or infant dedication (with the Service of Thanksgiving and Blessing) followed by Baptism (and Confirmation) after profession of faith.

This pattern is available in practice now in the Church of England but the presence and membership of those with baptist convictions could be affirmed. This provision of alternative patterns of initiation is operative in the United Reformed Church, in the Church of North India and Pakistan and in Areas of

Ecumenical Experiment. It is recommended in various recent writings by people of varying conviction and the *BEM* Report asks that serious consideration be given to it.

It is increasingly clear that many baptists are willing to accept the validity of infant baptism followed by later profession of faith. It is indiscriminate baptism not followed by nurture in faith or confession of faith which is the major stumbling block to full recognition and acceptance. On the other hand those who baptize infants will have to be assured that any form of 're-baptism' will be avoided. This is not an easy option. Families will have to decide which pattern of administration to follow. Any 're-baptism' of adults following an infant baptism would put an almost intolerable strain on the reciprocal relationship.

General and Discriminate baptism of infants

BEM has argued strongly against 'apparently indiscriminate' baptism and this is the main problem for many baptists on the one hand, and, on the other hand, others who wish to embrace positively infant baptism in the believing family. It is to be hoped that increasingly the Church of England will implement its present Canon Law and liturgical provision, and perhaps clarify the situation for those who (mistakenly) believe that indiscriminate baptism is the theological position or normal practice of the Church. Although for the past two decades the Church of England has managed to hold together parishes, clergy and people operating diverse policies of general and discriminate baptism, this is largely through lack of clear leadership from Bishops and General Synod. Biblical theology, the ecumenical situation and the secularism and multi-faith nature of contemporary society calls for a clear, discriminating pastoral policy. On that basis Christians will increasingly be able to move forward together with mutual confidence to shared mission, evangelism and the work of the kingdom of God.

There would be enthusiasm for and clarity about believing in baptism.

Almighty God,
who anointed Jesus at his baptism with the Holy Spirit
and revealed him as your beloved Son:
inspire us, your children,
who are born of water and the Spirit,
to surrender our lives to your service,
that we may rejoice to be called the sons of God;
through Jesus Christ our Lord.

Collect for Epiphany 1
[Alternative Service Book, p. 463]

Notes

Chapter 1

1 *Baptism, Eucharist and Ministry* (cited in future as *BEM*) Baptism III.8
2 *Services of Baptism and Confirmation*
3 Baptism IV.C.16
4 Thurian, *Ecumenical Perspectives on BEM*, p. 161
5 *ibid.*, p. 161
6 D. Barrett, *World Christian Encyclopaedia*, p. 9
7 See *BEM*, Baptism I;
M. Warren 'I believe in the Great Commission'
D. Watson 'I believe in evangelism'
E. Gibbs 'I believe in Church Growth'
as a few titles in the growing tide of books and resources on evangelism and church growth.
8 See C. O. Buchanan, *Adult Baptisms*, p. 3 and the Statistical Supplement to the Church of England Yearbook
9 *ARCIC Final Report*, p. 70

Chapter 2

1 Oscar Cullmann, *Baptism in the New Testament*
2 Eric Lane, *I want to be baptised*
3 *ibid.*, p. 28
4 Flemington, *The NT Doctrine of Baptism*, pp. 105ff
5 *ibid.*, p. 109
6 Sanday and Headlam, *Romans ICC*, p. 107
7 R. E. O. White, *The Biblical Doctrine of Initiation*, pp. 203 & 352ff
8 Beasley-Murray, *Baptism in the New Testament*, p. 247
9 Lane, p. 29

Chapter 3

1 *Bible and Theological Dictionaries*, art. Covenant
2 Beasley-Murray, *Baptism in the New Testament*, p. 334ff
3 *ibid.*, p. 341

Chapter 4

1 Arndt and Gingrich, *A Greek-English Lexicon of the New Testament*
2 I. H. Marshall, *The Meaning of the verb 'to baptize'*, Evangelical Quarterly, Vol. 45, No. 3, 1973
3 Cited in Beasley-Murray, *Baptism in the New Testament*, p. 17
4 The detailed evidence is conveniently found in Beasley-Murray, Flemington or Jeremias, *Infant baptism in the first four centuries*
5 Flemington, op. cit. p. 4
6 C. O. Buchanan, *A Case for Infant Baptism*, p. 14 n. 1
7 e.g. N. Geldenhuys, *The Gospel of Luke*, p. 140
8 see J. D. G. Dunn, *Baptism in the Holy Spirit*, p. 8ff and I. H. Marshall, *The Gospel of Luke*, p. 145ff on Luke 3.16
9 Dunn, op. cit. p. 10ff and Marshall, op. cit. p. 145ff

Chapter 5

1 as J. D. G. Dunn, *Baptism in the Holy Spirit*, chapter 3

Chapter 6

1 James Denney, *The Death of Christ*, p. 185
2 Beasley-Murray, *Baptism in the New Testament*, p. 272, n. 3
3 op. cit., p. 273
4 E. Lane, *I want to be Baptized*: J. D. G. Dunn, 'Baptism' *IBD*
5 *Ecclesiastical Polity Book 5*, p. 37, cited in Griffith Thomas, *The Principles of Theology*, p. 362
6 *BEM* III.8
7 A. M. Stibbs, *Baptism into Christ*, p. 11f
8 J. I. Packer, *I want to be a Christian*, p. 100
9 Letters of C. S. Lewis, ed. W. H. Lewis, Bles. 1966 p. 239
10 J. I Packer, *I want to be a Christian*, p. 94f
11 Session VII, Canon 8
12 cf. Augustine on 2 Timothy 2.20ff
13 J. C. S. Nias, *Gorham and the Bishop of Exeter*, SPCK, 1951, p. 98
14 V. Jack, *Believe and be Baptised*
15 Thurian, *Ecumenical Perspectives*, p. 161
16 Beasley-Murray, p. 273

Chapter 7

1 *BEM* IV C 16

Chapter 8

1 e.g. Watson, *Baptism not for Infants* and Beasley-Murray, *Baptism in the New Testament*

2 V. Jack, op. cit.

3 Beasley-Murray, op. cit. p. 361

4 op. cit. p. 376

5 J. K. Davies, *Babies, Believers and Baptism*, pp. 7, 19

6 Watson, op. cit. p. 86

Chapter 9

1 *BEM* Baptism IV C 16 and V 21

2 R. R. Osborn, *Forbid them not*, SPCK 1972

3 *The Canons of the Church of England*, Church Information Office 1981

4 Grove Books, 1982

5 SPCK, 1984

6 *Towards a Church of England response to BEM* and *ARCIC*, CIO, 1985

Chapter 10

1 Throughout this chapter I am indebted to an unpublished paper produced by a Working Party with Anglican, Methodist, United Reformed and Baptist members under the chairmanship of Mr Gordon Landreth of the Church of England Evangelical Council.

2 IVA 13

3 Baptist Union *Response of the Council to Baptism Eucharist and Ministry*

4 *BEM* 'Baptism Commentary' 21(b)

5 op. cit. p. 80

6 'Theological Renewal' Feb-Mar 1978 and C. O. Buchanan, *Adult Baptisms* p. 23f

7 C. O. Buchanan, op. cit. p. 24

8 C. O. Buchanan, *One Baptism Once*, p. 22

Chapter 11

1 *One Lord, One Baptism*, SCM 1961 p. 71

2 The Theology of the Sacraments and Other Papers 1957 p. 146 quoted in G. Ogilvie, *Preaching at Baptisms*, p. 5

3 *The Biblical Doctrine of Infant Baptism*, ET 1953 p. 236

4 Roger Lloyd, *The Church of England 1900–1965*, London 1966 p. 281

Bibliography

Arndt, W. F. and Gingrich F. W. *A Greek-English Lexicon of the New Testament* Cambridge 1957

Baillie, J. *Baptism & Conversion* OUP London 1964

Ball, P. *Journey into Faith* SPCK London 1984

Baptist Union *Response of the Council to Baptism, Eucharist & Ministry* London 1985

Barrett, C. K. *Church, Ministry and Sacraments* Paternoster Exeter 1985

Barth, K. *The Teaching of the Church regarding Baptism* (translated E. A. Payne) SCM London 1948

Beasley-Murray, G. R. *Baptism in the New Testament* Eerdmans Grand Rapids, Michigan 1962/1984

Beasley-Murray, G. R. *Baptism Today and Tomorrow* Macmillan London 1966

Beckwith, R. T. 'Infant Baptism' *New International Dictionary of New Testament Theology* edited C. Brown Paternoster Exeter 1975

Beckwith, R. T., Buchanan, C. O.; Prior, K. ed. *Services of Baptism and Confirmation* Marcham Abingdon 1967

Bridge, D. and Phypers, D. *The water that divides* IVP Leicester 1977

British Council of Churches: *Report of the Inter-church enquiry into Baptismal Practice, BCC London n.d.*

British Council of Churches: *One Lord, one Faith, one Baptism — guidelines and materials for inter-church worship* BCC London n.d.

Bromiley, G. *Children of Promise* Eerdmans Grand Rapids 1979

Buchanan, C. O. *Baptismal Discipline* Grove Nottingham 1972/4

Buchanan, C. O. *A Case for Infant Baptism* Grove Nottingham 1973

Buchanan, C. O. *Adult Baptisms* Grove Nottingham 1985

Buchanan, C. O. ed. *Evangelical Essays on Church and Sacraments* SPCK London 1972

Buchanan, C. O. *Policies for Infant Baptism* Grove Nottingham 1987

Buchanan, C. O. *One Baptism once* Grove Nottingham 1978

Buchanan, C. O. *ARCIC and LIMA on Baptism and Eucharist* Grove Nottingham 1983

Burnish, R. *The Meaning of Baptism* SPCK London 1985

Carey, G. 'Christian Beginning', chapter 5 of *Obeying Christ in a Changing World* ed. J. R. W. Stott, Vol. 1. *The Lord Christ* Collins Glasgow 1977

Carr, W. *Brief Encounters* SPCK London 1985

Craston, R. C. *Baptism* BCMS London n.d.

Crowe, P. *Christian Baptism* Mowbray Oxford 1980

Cullmann, O. *Baptism in the New Testament* (translated by J. K. S. Reid) SCM London 1950

Davies, J. K. *Babies, Believers and Baptism* Grace London 1983

Dunn, J. D. G. *Baptism in the Holy Spirit* SCM London 1970

Dunn, J. D. G. 'Baptism' *The Illustrated Bible Dict*. IVP Leicester 1980

Eastman, A. T. *The Baptizing Community* Seabury Minnesota 1982

Ely Report *Christian Initiation — Birth and Growth in the Christian Society* CIO London 1971

Faith and Order Advisory Group (Board for Mission and Unity) *Toward a Church of England Response to BEM and ARCIC* CIO London 1985

Flemington, W. F. *The New Testament Doctrine of Baptism* SPCK London 1948/1957

Forsyth, P. T. *The Church and the Sacraments* Independent London 1917/1947

Gilmore, A. ed. *Christian Baptism* Lutterworth London 1959

Gilmore, A *Baptism and Christian Unity* Lutterworth London 1966

Green, E. M. B. *I believe in the Holy Spirit* Hodder London 1975

Griffith Thomas, W. H. *The Principles of theology* Church Book Room Press London 1930/63

Hart, G. *Right to Baptize* Hodder London 1966

Hoad, J. *The Baptist* Grace London 1986

Hulse, E. *The Testimony of Baptism* Carey Haywards Heath 1982

Jack, V. *Believe and be Baptised* 1970

Jeremias, J. *Infant Baptism in the First Four Centuries* SCM London 1960

Jewett, P. K. *Infant baptism and the covenant of grace* Eerdmans Grand Rapids 1978

Kingdon, D. *Children of Abraham* Walter Worthing 1973

Knaresborough Report *Communion before Confirmation*? CIO London 1985

Lampe, G. W. H. *The Seal of the Spirit* SPCK London 1951/67

Lane, E. *I want to be Baptised* Grace London 1986

Marcel, P. *The Biblical Doctrine of Infant Baptism* (translated — P. E. Hughes) 1951/1953

Marshall, I. H. *Luke — Historian and Theologian* Paternoster Exeter 1970

Marshall, I. H. *The Meaning of the Verb 'to Baptize'* Evangelical Quarterly Vol. 45, No. 3. 1973

Martin, R. P. *Worship in the early Church* Marshalls London 1964

Moody, D. *Baptism: Foundation for Christian Unity* Westminister Press Philadelphia 1967

Moore, G. and Briden, T. *Moore's Introduction to English Canon Law* Mowbray Oxford 1985

Moss, B. S. ed. *Crisis for Baptism* SCM London 1965

Motyer, J. A. *Baptism in the Book of Common Prayer* FEC Leicester 1962

Motyer, J. A. 'Baptism', *The New Bible Dict.*, ed. J. D. Douglas IVP London 1962

Moule, C. F. D. *Worship in the New Testament* Lutterworth London 1961

Moynagh, M. 'Home to Home: Towards a Biblical Model of the Family' *Anvil*, Vol. 3. No. 3, 1986

Murray, J. *Christian Baptism* Philadelphia 1952

Ogilvie, G. *Preaching at Baptism* Grove Nottingham 1979

Osborn, R. R. *Forbid them not* SPCK London 1972

Packer, J. I. *I want to be a Christian* Kingsway Eastbourne 1977

Pawson, D. and Buchanan, C. O. *Infant Baptism under Cross-examination* Grove Nottingham 1974

Price, Tony *Evangelical Anglicans and the Lima Text* Grove Nottingham 1985

Quick, O. C. *The Christian Sacraments* Nisbet London 1927/1932

Richardson, A. 'Initiation, Christian' in *A Dictionary of Christian Theology* edited A. Richardson, SCM London 1969

Robinson, D. W. B. *The Meaning of Baptism* Falcon London 1956

Scotland, Church of *The Biblical Doctrine of Baptism* St Andrew Edinburgh 1958

Silversides, M. *Folk Religion: Friend or Foe?* Grove Nottingham 1986

Southwell Diocesan Working Party *Report on policies concerning Infant Baptism* Grove Nottingham 1977

Stibbs, A. M. *Understanding the Sacraments* Falcon London 1960

Stibbs, A. M. *Baptism into Christ* Falcon London 1960

Stott, J. R. W. 'The Evangelical Doctrine of Baptism' Ch. 6 of *The Anglican Synthesis* ed. by W. R. F. Browning, Peter Smith Derby 1964

Thurian, M. *Ecumenical Perspectives on Baptism, Eucharist and Ministry* WCC Geneva 1983

Wainwright, G. *Christian Initiation* Lutterworth London 1969

Watson, T. E. *Baptism not for Infants* 1962

Whitaker, E. C. *Sacramental Initiation complete in Baptism* Grove Nottingham 1975

White, R. E. O. *The Biblical Doctrine of Initiation* Hodder London 1960

William, R. R. 'Baptism' in *A Theological Wordbook of the Bible* Edited A. Richardson, SCM London 1960

World Council of Churches Commission on Faith and Order *One Lord, One Baptism* SCM London 1960

World Council of Churches Faith and Order Paper 111 *Baptism, Eucharist and Ministry* (The Lima text) WCC Geneva 1982

Wright, D. F. *Baptism, Eucharist and Ministry — an evangelical assessment* Rutherford Forum Paper Edinburgh 1984

Index to Subjects and Authors

Index of Bible References